rock bottom is a *beautiful* place 3

LIVING WITH A GRATEFUL HEART

Diane Cunningham

THE ROCK BOTTOM SERIES™

Rock Bottom Is A Beautiful Place 3: Living with a Grateful Heart
© 2015 Diane Cunningham

For more information, please email info@nacwe.org.

Published by:
Diane Cunningham
2140 E Southlake Blvd, Suite L-643
Southlake, TX 76092

ISBN-10: 1937660699
ISBN-13: 978-1-937660-69-7
eBook ISBN: 978-1-937660-70-3

Scriptures marked KJV are taken from the King James Version of the Bible. In the public domain.

Scriptures marked NIV are taken from the Holy Bible, NEW INTERNATIONAL VERSION®, NIV® Copyright © 1973, 1978, 1984, 2011 by Biblica, Inc.® Used by permission. All rights reserved worldwide.

Scriptures marked ESV are taken from the ESV® Bible (The Holy Bible, English Standard Version®), copyright © 2001 by Crossway, a publishing ministry of Good News Publishers. Used by permission. All rights reserved.

Scriptures marked NLT are taken from the Holy Bible, New Living Translation, copyright ©1996, 2004, 2007, 2013 by Tyndale House Foundation. Used by permission of Tyndale House Publishers, Inc., Carol Stream, Illinois 60188. All rights reserved.

CONTENTS

ACKNOWLEDGMENTS

Thank you to all of the Rock Bottom fans who have read our first two books in the *Rock Bottom* series and followed us on our fan page!

Thank you, God, for the gift of desperation that leads us to where You need us and allows testimonies to be turned into triumphs.

To the gifted (and hilarious) editor for this book and all of the Rock Bottom books, Hanne Moon, for walking this delicate path with me and honoring our stories. We are so thankful for how you help us to craft words that get to the heart of the matter!

To the Rock Bottom Sisterhood, the women who are in books one, two, and three—you are my soul sisters, and we have walked through the coals together! I am honored to call you my friends and comrades for the journey.

To my family, friends, and colleagues who have known me during my Rock Bottom journey. Thank you for never letting me fall into believing that I was not capable or worthy of moving forward!

To all who have walked through any type of Rock Bottom, we hear you. We get you. We are you!

Thank you for the magnificent gift of grace.

To those still hurting, wandering, and wondering...welcome home. You are loved!

INTRODUCTION

Rock Bottom has many shapes and forms. Sometimes it happens in a split second; other times, it is a slow decent for years. It can happen in private or in public.

Pain is pain.

The *Rock Bottom Is A Beautiful Place* books are filled with the stories of women that have known darkness. They have seen the inside of despair, of hospital rooms, of sanitariums, of treatment centers, and the bathroom floor in a heap of tears.

As I have walked through the past two years of my recovery journey, I have learned so much from the process. It had nothing to do with the alcohol and had everything to do with life. It was about my inner fear and my seemingly endless hunger for love. I understand that now.

Beauty and gratitude can be found in the ugliest of places. It is a matter of perspective and seeing with new eyes. I have found the best moments of my life are small little moments that are big when I look in the rearview mirror.

Moments of clarity.

Moments of understanding who I am and how to share my feelings out loud.

Moments of recognition of grief and letting the feelings wash over me in waves.

Moments of seeing how my story is the same as so many others—the circumstances just look different.

We are all broken, my friends. We are all only saved by the grace of God. We all have rock bottom days and events. We all have to walk through tragedies and triumphs.

Be willing to ask for help.

Be willing to stop pretending.

Be willing to give up so you can gain it all.

This *Rock Bottom* book is just as magnificent as the first two.

Stories of grief, rape, deception, death, and loss of innocence. Heartbreak. Stories of women who saw the end of the rope and realized it was Jesus they had to hold onto. I am in awe. I am one of these women, and I proudly walk side by side with them.

As I said in the first two *Rock Bottom* books:

Rock bottom is rock bottom. It is tragic and ugly, and I felt utterly horrified at myself on that day. But that day and that disgust finally got me willing to consider that I might have a problem. And then willing enough to be humble and ask for help. As it so eloquently states in the "big book" of Alcoholics Anonymous: "All of us felt at times that we were gaining control, but such intervals—usually brief—were inevitably followed by still less control, which led in time to pitiful and incomprehensible demoralization."

God set me free that day too. And I'm so very grateful for my rock bottom.

What is Rock Bottom?

Rock Bottom looks different for each of us. You will see that as you read through these stories. This book is a movement. It is women sharing things they have never shared before. It is full of pain and purpose, tragedy and turning points. As I've read through each story submitted, I've sat and cried.

Once again, I stand in awe of how these books have come to life. I pray for courage for each woman as we keep walking side by side. I wholeheartedly know that God's grace sets us free.

This book is a testimony...my testimony and the testimony of many.

The miracles are in each day, in each story, in each woman. I think too often we keep "looking," "searching," and "hunting" for more...without realizing that the MORE is never out there. You never get there. You never graduate. You are always in process.

We want to hear from you after you read it. That is the gift you can give back to us.

If you are tempted to judge us, you are in the wrong place.

We don't need judgment and neither do you. We've walked through that and have already endured plenty of it from our own negative self-talk and the judgments of others. If you are here to support another broken soul that is loved by God, stay around.

To those of you that are still hiding, running, and hoping no one will see how broken you are...

I understand. It was me too. I know that sharing this message is controversial. I know that you might want to judge me. I challenge you NOT to. I encourage you to think before you do that. I am just like you. I am just willing to share my message in a BIG public way. I feel that this is what God has asked me to do.

Share with Us

Every woman has a story. We know you have a story too. We invite you to come and join us as you rise up victorious. Share your message. Speak your truth. Stop hiding.

This is the last book in our Rock Bottom series, but we have plans for other things in the works. We know that God loves to keep surprising us.

We plan to continue sharing a message of our experiences, strengths, and hope. We would love for you to come with us...

Get signed up for our emails and updates over on our website or our fan page. Find out more here:

www.rockbottomisabeautifulplace.com
www.facebook.com/rockbottomisabeautifulplace

Are you a Christian businesswoman who would like to have the fellowship and support of fellow Christian women entrepreneurs? Visit us at www.nacwe.org to join the fastest growing network of women just like you.

Are you a businesswoman looking for a safe place to connect with fellow sisters of faith who understand the obstacles and challenges you face on a daily basis? Visit www.nacwe.org and discover the rich network of friends and resources that are available to you.

Are you walking through your own Rock Bottom and need some encouragement and support? Visit http://rockbottomisabeautifulplace.com/rock-bottom-gift/and sign up to get our FREE GIFT to you.

LIVING WITH A
GRATEFUL HEART

Diane Cunningham

Whatever we are waiting for—peace of mind, contentment, grace, the inner awareness of simple abundance—it will surely come to us, but only when we are ready to receive it with an open and grateful heart.

– Sarah Ban Breathnach

Gratitude is my default setting. For this I am truly grateful. (See...there I go again.)

My heart was broken during the writing of this book. The amazing thing is that the heart is so resilient. It wants so much to heal. It goes to work quickly on healing itself and it learns to beat again.

But this brings me to the endless list of questions in my head:

- What does it mean to live with a grateful heart?
- When your heart has been broken, how do you recover?
- How do you forgive?
- How do you trust again?
- How do you embrace the good and the horrible?
- Why did this happen? Why?

I have wandered around my house a lot lately, saying out loud: "Why? Why? Why?" Often we will never know why. We must stop asking "Why?" because it just leads to more mind torture. Most of the time, the reasons are NOT for us to know. We have no control over other people and their actions. We have no control over how they treat our precious and vulnerable heart. We only have control over how we respond.

This is a story about love, but it is NOT a love story.

It is a story about walking through endings and NOT getting stuck there.

It is a story about forgiveness and of passionately pursuing peace.

I have had many rock bottoms in my life. My last drink and my alcoholism came to light in 2013. A decade before that, I lost my career and counseling license. And in between, I walked through the end of my ten-year marriage in 2011. You can read about the first stories in the original *Rock Bottom Is a Beautiful Place* and in *Rock Bottom Is A Beautiful Place: Living Your Calling*. This story is about love, marriage, and relationships... but ultimately, it is a story about me loving me.

Let's start with the marriage

My marriage looked good from the outside. We were both good Christians that went to church and loved the Lord. I was his second wife. We spent ten years holding it together with friendship and Band-Aids. We were survivors holding onto life rafts with each other. We walked through deaths, my lawsuit, infertility, military moves, career changes, deployments, and all of the regular life issues. We kept trying. We held on.

During the course of our marriage, we spent five of the ten years in marriage counseling. We attended group marriage intensives. We went to church. We read books. What I know now is that there was a secret lying below the surface that was fighting a waging war no matter what we did.

As 2011 began, things started to crumble again for us. We had been married for almost ten years. We had trouble for many years and in 2008, we separated for six months. Then we reconciled after some much-needed truth spilled out about addictions hidden under the surface. We got down to gut level truth. One of the things I remember saying is, "I would rather have the worst truth than a lie." We reconnected, recommitted, and renewed our vows in 2009 and moved back in together. Things were going much better and life was moving along. And then things began to drift again. Rock bottom is often a slow drift, a seeping in of sadness, an empty crevasse that you are not sure how to fix.

During that same spring, my business was in fast motion too. I was in the middle of writing my first compilation book in February and March, *Inspired Women Succeed*. We were preparing to host the first national conference for the National Association of Christian Women Entrepreneurs that was scheduled for April. And in the midst of this, Robert and I also survived a plane crash on March 23rd. The plane was totaled and we both survived.

To say things were a bit stressful is an understatement. During all of this craziness, our marriage was becoming more and more strained. Threads were holding us together. And within two weeks after the NACWE conference, the divorce paperwork had been filed. The conversations had been had with the counselor and our pastor. I will never forget the day that I took off my wedding rings in the Presbyterian church after we met for a session with our pastor. After the things that were spoken that day, I could not continue wearing my rings.

Then the Divorce

Things moved quickly...seventy-six days later, it was final on July 29th. Garage sale, moving us both to new locations. Twelve years on the record books. And time for me to start healing.

Over the next weeks and months, I read books, wrote in my journal, cried, and started painting my Heart Art by Diane. I went to divorce recovery, met with a female counselor, worked on me with the tools I had from my experience as a counselor and as a woman who had been to many, many counselors over the course of twenty years. I felt my feelings. I drowned some of them in my wine bottles. I avoided some of them with business and workaholic tendencies.

In addition to this, I had to say goodbye to my beloved dog Bear in 2012 after thirteen years of companionship. During these years, I began drinking more. Every night the alcohol was my companion. I worked all day trying to hold my business together, and every night I would look forward to my strawberry margaritas or my bottle of wine.

This is not a story about my ex-husband; it is the story of how gratitude is found in every single thing. He has his story and I have mine. We are friends and I wish him every happiness. I see no other way of living that would make sense to me. He is remarried and I am happy for him. I am single again once more after one relationship.

The miracle of these years is that I was very quickly able to forgive and be at peace. I chose to look for the good. I chose to move forward. I know that I was masking a lot of my pain with the drinking, shopping, and business...but I also know that I was (and still am) grateful for every lesson learned.

Then I started the endless dating

Rock bottom is a beautiful place because no matter what your relationship status is, you are loved.

I began the process of dating through online dating sites and chance encounters. It was rather dismal and depressing. Dating apps, singles websites...I have tried them all. I would go on and off. I would go on dates. I would get my hopes up.

Just to give you a sneak peek:

- There was the red dress first date on Valentine's Day where I drove two hours to Oklahoma...not my best move.

- There was the guy who admitted over coffee that he ate dog food.

- There was the one who did not have a job and did not seem to think that was an issue in any way.

- The man who wanted me to sit on his lap in Starbucks five minutes after we met for the first time—we can just call him Santa Claus.

- The one with the eye patch.

- The one who was late because he had to run errands and took a nap.

- And this is just a small sampling~~~

Once I got sober, I did what was suggested and didn't date for a year. But then I was up and at it again. In 2014 I was on a mission. I started keeping track as I went along. I went on twenty-nine first dates. Yes, you read that right. Twenty-nine different men. I learned so much.

I had more than one date with some of them, but most only made it for one coffee or dinner. That was plenty. I learned about men and all that was out there in the Dallas area. I learned about what worked for me. And most of all, I learned what did NOT work for me at all.

Throughout this time, I walked daily in gratitude. I did finally get to my limit on a weekend in November when I was texting with twelve different guys and felt like I was losing my mind. I gave up. I turned all of the apps off. I went off the grid. And I honestly felt like I was going through a detox. Those first few days were rough, and then I felt the freedom of trusting God's timing completely. That God knows who my future husband is and that I don't need to run all around Dallas looking for him.

Months before this breaking point, in February of 2014, I had sat down and written out a dating manifesto. I still have it in two locations that I see daily—on the bulletin board behind my desk and in my kitchen—laminated and sitting on a cookbook stand.

Diane's Dating Manifesto

I will NOT chase, pursue, manipulate, fix, finagle, or hunt down someone to be with me. Dating is not HUNTING!

I AM WORTHY of being pursued.

I AM WORTHY of LOVE.

I AM ENOUGH.

My quirks, emotions, and life are NOT WRONG. I am who I am. It is OK!

I AM LOVEABLE.

I AM BEAUTIFUL.

I AM WILLING TO WAIT.

God created Me. And what is meant for me...cannot be lost.

Written February 2014

After turning off the apps in November of 2014 and trusting that God would take care of me and introduce me to who He wanted me to meet, I felt a peace. I had finally gotten to a place of surrender. The place I had found once before after I asked for help with my drinking.

My first relationship

It was a few weeks later that I reconnected through Facebook with a friend from high school. We began talking and texting in December and saw each other for the first time in twenty-three years during Christmas of 2014 when I went on a pre-planned trip to see my family.

Thus began my first dating relationship after divorce. We dated long distance. We prayed by Skype and phone. When we could, we visited each other in person in California and in Texas.

We were in what looked like a fairy tale of love, happy selfies, fun adventures, and rekindled youth. Until it didn't. The story is fresh and I want to focus on my part of it and not betray a story that is not mine to share.

The relationship ended on June 21st during the final days of the writing of this book. I chose to end it for valid reasons that did not agree with who I am and how I live my life. It has been a very painful few weeks of letting go, asking WHY, and rethinking the past six months.

In the depths of this, I am watching myself live in total gratitude.

I am in pain and yet, full of hope.

I am thankful for all that I have learned and how I have walked with grace and dignity through this.

Living with a Grateful Heart

- I am grateful that God did for me what I could not have done for myself.

- I am grateful that I was willing to have a relationship and a "boyfriend" for the first time.

- I am grateful that God's timing was impeccable on the ending and how it played out.

- I am grateful that I was willing to be loved and give love...to be vulnerable.

- I am grateful that I stood up for me and said what needed to be said.

- I am truly, truly grateful.

And now I am once again single. I am full of gratitude for that also. I know that God has a plan for me and that He has a man for me that is called to be my husband. I know that God is providing for me the training ground to learn what I do want and what I do NOT want.

No matter what, there is always something to be grateful for. We always have a choice to look for the good or the lesson.

When I was going through the end of my ten-year marriage, I felt like I would never find happiness again. I questioned the process, my journey.

I questioned God, and His plan for me. I rarely question Him now, because I know deep down that He always knows best.

Living with a grateful heart is about honoring the daily process of learning.

It is about knowing that God has me right where He needs me today. That I am NOT running late even when I think that I am. That He is always in control.

Rock Bottom is a beautiful place because He loves me so much and meets me there every single time!! God's timing is impeccable.

THE PERFECT PLACE TO BEGIN AGAIN AND AGAIN

Elise Adams

Every good and perfect gift is from above, coming down from the Father of the heavenly lights, who does not change like shifting shadows.

– James 1:17 (NIV)

My Rock Bottom experience led me to living with a grateful heart by teaching me how little it takes to survive. Since then I've been living with an abundance of blessings poured out in "...good measure, pressed down, shaken together and running over" (Luke 6:38 NIV).

Those blessings weren't always so obvious, however.

Nearly eight years ago, I spent three years homeless and in an abusive relationship. During those years, I gave birth to two precious girls without prenatal care, vitamins, rest, or a safe home. And that's not to mention the endless days I spent hungry, scared, and very alone.

Imagine my surprise when I found myself at a new rock bottom just last September. After rebuilding a life, marrying a new man, and having a precious little boy together, everything was crashing down around me again. The man who I'd thought was the answer to all those lonely, scared, helpless days was living a double life that I couldn't ignore any longer.

I'll never forget packing up only what would fit in my truck, telling the kids we were leaving, and driving off into the Arizona sunset. It was hours before I could even cry. The freeway I traveled was the same freeway I'd driven with a just-born Michaela all those years ago, homeless, trapped, and afraid. And it felt so strange to chase the same storm clouds across the desert as I left behind all my new hopes and dreams.

How had this happened again? How had I chosen so terribly wrong... again? My devastation and shame were so deep I couldn't even imagine there was an alternative.

What was completely different on this mad dash out of town, however, was that this time I went with my hands firmly in the hands of my Heavenly Father. Instead of wasting years in emptiness and desperation, this time I knew exactly where I was going. Even though I was once again homeless and jobless, I wasn't without a foundation to stand tall on.

This time I knew I wasn't alone. Not really.

When Michaela was just nine months old, I hadn't prayed in over two years. Every time I left the girls' dad (only to go back to him and our crime-driven, fearful, and angry homeless life), I knew that I was sacrificing my soul. It was a betrayal of everything God had done for me. How could I keep praying when I continued to betray my God and myself every day?

See, I'd first met my best friend Jesus Christ as a child. I'll always remember going up to the chapel at one of the seven schools I attended in just three years of formal schooling to pour out my heart to Him. I called it "talking to God" because "praying" seemed like I had to be perfect first. But in those talks I cried, screamed, asked Him "why" He'd given me an abusive father and a crazy mom. And He answered me. Every time.

But after I lost my daughter while walking through mental illness and prescription pill addiction, and when all my attempts at doing the right thing seemed to bring me back to more loneliness, I didn't see any reason to keep trying. I walked away from everything.

My family.

My daughter.

And God.

So that night I wasn't crying out for help while my beautiful nine-month-old Michaela slept on a makeshift bed on the floor of our hotel room. I didn't come to the end of myself and finally turn back. I'd stopped crying out long before. How could I ask God for help when I refused to stick with any of the many second chances He'd given me?

Often during those years I recalled the sermon illustration of the man who'd made it to heaven only to complain to God that He hadn't rescued him from the rooftop of his house during a flood. God replied, "Did you see the helicopter I sent? What about the boat with the rescue workers? The raft that bumped into your house? You didn't see any of those?" To which the humbled man replied, "But I was waiting for You!"

Since I hadn't taken any of the boats, helicopters, rescue personnel, or other exit ramps off the crazy slide of a homeless life, how could I keep calling out to Him?

All I was doing that night was flipping through the channels because I couldn't sleep. As I switched through the channels, I almost missed it. The channel read TBN, and I never watched Trinity Broadcasting Network. Their over-the-top brand of Christianity never felt helpful to me. But these scenes of bucolic, peaceful, rolling hills were way more surprising than the loud, boisterousness I usually skipped right past on this channel.

So, after scrolling past the surprising scene, I reversed direction and switched back to the channel. The documentary commentator was quietly narrating as the camera panned over some gently rolling terrain and settled on a tiny, whitewashed chapel topped by an Orthodox cross. The montage continued with scenes from inside the small chapel and included icons of Christ. I gasped and burst into tears. What a strange scene to pop on the screen. And from the Trinity Broadcasting Network no less...what was this?

To this day I don't know exactly what the documentary or program was that I saw that night. What I won't ever forget is the conversation God and I had through my tears.

"It's too late. I can't go back now."

"You know better. It is never too late."

"But what do I do? I've tried again and again and again. I don't know what to do anymore."

And into my mind, instantly, came the moment from years before when one of the two people who'd never given up on me had taught me the Jesus prayer. "When you don't know what to say, when you don't know what to do, simply repeat the Jesus prayer. 'Jesus Christ, have mercy on me, a sinner.'"

Now, driving across the Arizona desert with the kids falling asleep in my rearview mirror, facing the end of another relationship and the loss of all my newly rebuilt dreams, and with tears finally streaming down my face, I knew exactly what to do. I didn't know where I was going to live, or how I was going to support myself, or how I could possibly be a strong single mom, but I knew Who to talk to about it.

Over the next few days, several families stepped up to love us through this hard time. That very night a precious family invited us to spend the weekend at their home in central California. And my Celebrate Recovery family back in our hometown opened their arms to us. For a full month, the kids and I stayed in the spare room of my accountability partner and her husband. Starting again at the very bottom was nearly paralyzing, but as a great friend of mine told me, "You'll never truly be homeless again. You're just houseless for a moment."

I took that statement as the lifeline that it was, and I started knocking on every door possible. The church school my kids had gone to previously welcomed the girls back in and the Christian afterschool center did the same for my little boy. I began accepting any job I could find.

And once again my Provider, Protector, and Friend truly cared for us. Within one month a parish family rented us our first new home. I was employed full time, and not just at any old job, but with two clients who appreciated my independent spirit. This allowed me to be home with the kids if they were sick or struggling without missing work.

Ever since that new rock bottom, I've learned that gratitude compounds with every blessing and praise I credit to my Heavenly Father. People talk about "peeling the onion" when it comes to recovery and healing. Well, I've discovered that God loves to wrap me in layers of Love that can never be peeled away, no matter what circumstances bottom me out! I'll never again have to run so far away to prove His love for me. He rescued my soul after I'd rejected Him and turned from Him completely for years! And He's rebuilt my life from the ground up in just a few short months after another humbling rock bottom.

In fact, this next week the kids and I move into my dream home after eight months in this tiny miracle apartment! No, I am not a lottery winner nor have I sold a startup. This house is a beautiful rental home that I'd first dreamt of living in when we lived next door to it several years back. As soon as the "silly" dream came to mind, I put it to rest though. After all, this particular "dream home" was our friends' personal home!

Imagine my surprise when I got the email asking me if we were looking for a bigger place.

Today I know that no matter how hard I try, I will still fail and fall sometimes. And when I do, I can turn around instantly and stand tall, forgiven and free on the Foundation bigger and stronger than anything that trips me up. And that same Foundation I stand on loves to give good gifts to His children. Today I know that receiving those gifts is one of the ways I glorify Him.

Everything I have is a gift from God. And that is *all* I need.

Elise Adams is a single mom of four children with three little ones still at home. She lives on the dry side of Washington State where she enjoys reading, gardening, and entrepreneuring. You can learn more about her writing and speaking at EliseWrites.com.

ABORTION— LEGAL?

Terri Baxter

Blessed be the God and Father of our Lord Jesus Christ, the Father of mercies and God of all comfort, who comforts us in all our affliction, so that we may be able to comfort those who are in any affliction, with the comfort with which we ourselves are comforted by God.

– 2 Cor. 1:3,4 (ESV)

In 1973, Roe vs. Wade was passed and abortion became legal. I was just graduating from high school, entering the "time of my life." Off to college

I went and met the man of my young dreams. The following year I found myself pregnant and scared. My boyfriend absolutely did not want to have a child. I was embarrassed that I was pregnant and unmarried and had to tell my Christian parents. He suggested abortion. He said we wouldn't have to tell, and no one would ever know. Though I was a Christian, I was afraid of the future and had never really thought about abortion until that moment. I finally decided to have one by convincing myself that I couldn't embarrass my family by being an unwed mother.

Besides, if abortion was so wrong, why was it legal?

I don't remember a lot of the details of that day, but I do remember the silence and fear in the waiting room. Everything was so matter-of-fact in the way they were doing business throughout the building. I was scared and numb. I was supposed to be strong, but on the inside, I was terrified. I remember the noise of the machine during the procedure, sounding like a vacuum cleaner. There was pain and then it was over. The nurse took me to recovery and then released me to go. I didn't shed a tear because that would have been a sign of weakness. I think I was in shock at the reality of what had just taken place.

I never mentioned this day to anyone.

I felt alone because I knew no one else around me would have made the choice I did or understand why. I was empty inside because I had taken away a potential future that would never be. I felt abandoned. After all, who could really love me if they knew what I had done?

However, life continued on. A few years went by, and I married my boyfriend (the man I had chosen abortion with). We had two children, and it was with the second one that the journey to Rock Bottom began.

My husband and I had a rocky marriage from the beginning. How could a marriage really survive when the foundation was built on secrets and silence? However, I was determined to make things work between us. But when I saw my first ultrasound while pregnant with my second child, looking at the tiny head, body, fingers, and toes, that's when those silent emotions I had kept at bay started to surface. Yes, I was excited to see the baby in my womb, but at the same time, feelings of shame, guilt, and horror manifested themselves.

What had I done eight years ago? I saw my tiny baby and had to face the fact (no more denying) that I had aborted a child, not a blob of tissue. I continued to suffer in silence because this was not a subject that was brought up in our home.

Three years after this moment, I found myself going through a divorce with two small children. I was broken and hit rock bottom. Through this darkness, I surrendered my life to the Lord to take control. I had been a Christian since the fifth grade, but I had been making life decisions on my own and asking God to bless them instead of following His will for my life. Although the pain of the divorce was immense, it wasn't until several years later that I came to understand I was grieving the loss of everything tied to that relationship—the loss of an unborn child, the end of a marriage, the end of future dreams as a family, and more.

Through this time in my life, I learned that God was always with me, always ready to restore my hope, and always ready to use me if I would just surrender. After going through a time of healing with the help of pastors, Divorce Care, Bible studies, and of course, alone time with God, I began feeling whole again. The pieces of my life felt like they were being put back together.

Through this journey, I learned some hard lessons:

- Just because something is legal, doesn't mean that it's right, especially in the eyes of God.
- "It is easier to obey God than disobey"—Rick Ferguson
- You can choose your choice, but you can't choose the consequences.
- 2 Cor. 1:3-4—God is the God of all comfort so we can comfort others...
- God took my ashes and turned them into beauty.

Only by God's grace and healing can I say I have been living with a grateful heart the last twenty-three years of my life. My life took a new direction after the start of my restoration. I remarried (God chose a wonderful, loving man for me), and I really believe if I hadn't gone through my divorce, I would not appreciate this wonderful and loving man, or have enjoyed our marriage in the way I do. I am forever telling people: "I chose the first one and God chose the second!" We have led Divorce Care groups for over fifteen years together, and we have watched God reconcile marriages, heal singles, and let people know they are loved when they are feeling the most unloved.

Even with all the restoration God has brought to my life, I had never openly discussed my abortion. Years had gone by, and I was remarried, raising my children, and attending a wonderful church. I had fought Stage 1 breast cancer and won. I felt like I had my spiritual life coming together until one Sunday when the pastor was preaching on obedience, and he opened time for people to give their testimonies. From far across the church, a young woman stood up and asked the church to forgive her of her sin of abortion.

I felt the Holy Spirit prompting me to surrender my abortion and bring it to light, but my heart started pounding and I started arguing with the Holy Spirit in my head. *What good could come from this? People will think I'm horrible!* I wanted to believe that the subject of abortion was over, ancient history, but I continued to feel the Holy Spirit's prompting that there was some unfinished business. *I don't want anyone to know my deepest darkest sin! I will lose my friends and I will never be able to serve in church or ministry again.*

The pastor was giving an altar call, so I thought God just wanted me to be obedient, go down front, and silently pray about my past abortion. I grabbed a friend who knew nothing of my past and asked her to pray with me. She encouraged me to talk to a pastor after we prayed. I said, "I don't think so!" She commented that I might be able to help someone, but again I said, "Ha! I don't think so!"

I finally gave in, but it didn't end there. The pastor wanted me to tell my story publicly. Again, I refused. Why would I want to tell my story in front of a church with 1500 or more pair of eyes and ears listening and watching? I felt like there were millions of people there.

"What if you could help one woman?" my pastor asked me. While I again refused, I felt that this was what God wanted me to do. In the end, my testimony to the church was this: "Everyone has secrets, and I want to publicly lay my secret sin of abortion at the cross. I want to surrender it for God to use if He chooses to."

After surrendering my secret, I think the most surprising thing that day was the response I received from the women. God blessed me with what seemed like all the women of the church coming forward to pray over me. I felt the weight of the silence and the shame and the guilt I had been carrying for years lifted off my shoulders and the peace from God settling onto them.

There was no more shame. Little did I know the Rock Bottom place of abortion would start me on a journey of ministering and coaching women to freedom and restoration.

I was not excited about telling my story of abortion because at the time, it was still not a subject that was openly talked about. However, when I was in a meeting and a woman stood up and angrily said, "My daughter had an abortion and we have to stop these women from killing these babies!," I knew she spoke the truth. But I also knew that God had not treated me with anger. Instead, He had treated me with love, compassion, comfort, and grace. He met me where I was, with open arms to receive me and to restore me. That was when I knew I would be taking an active part in telling how God wanted to restore other hurting women who suffered in silence and shame.

One of the first experiences I had was when I was the director of a pregnancy resource center that helped women in a crisis pregnancy. I thought I was teaching my volunteers to give pregnancy tests, read the results, and offer life-affirming options to the women that walked through our doors. Little did I know that the volunteers came through those same doors with hurts of their own, that they had been in hiding and holding onto their own pain. My heart hurt because, if the volunteers weren't living in the freedom of God's healing, how could they tell the women off the street they could trust God with the crisis they were in? I wanted these women to be able to experience the forgiveness, healing, restoration, and freedom that God had bestowed on me. I was once again grateful that I had gone through the depths of my past so God could use me to give hope to hurting women—to see a new glow on a woman's face, the heaviness lifted off her heart, or a new ministry or purpose begun. These are the things that keep me telling my story.

Through the past several years, I have been blessed at being used as a vessel to show God's grace. God has allowed me to see hundreds of women find their voice and to finally speak the truth of their pain.

I am silent no more.

Terri's Rock Bottom life experiences have been turned into opportunities for God to use in ministry. Terri is a Certified Life and Recovery Coach, is the former founder and director of Riverside Pregnancy Center in Denver, Colorado, and is on staff of the International Helpline for Abortion Recovery, which is available 24/7 for women hurting and recovering from abortion or thinking about choosing abortion. If you need help, call 1-866-482-LIFE or go to www.internationalhelpline.org

FOREVER LOVE

Kelly Bell

Yes, you can lose somebody overnight. Yes, your whole life can be turned upside down. Life is short. It can come and go like a feather in the wind.

– Shania Twain

How do you define hitting rock bottom? I think for everyone it's different as we all have different stories. For me, I hit rock bottom when I lost my husband in 2007. A part of me died with him. Through hitting rock bottom,

I have come to find one of my greatest gifts—strength—and I have grown so much more than I ever thought possible, even with all the struggles.

I met my husband, Joseph, in middle school and he quickly became one of my very best friends. We grew up with our friends as typical teenagers do. Several years into our friendship, we grew closer. Our relationship developed into much more and we started dating. Joe and I had such a heartfelt connection, I just knew deep down inside that he was the one. We had so much fun, and we really enjoyed being together and doing things as a couple. I think it was easy to see we were young and totally in love.

A few years went by and we became pregnant with our first child. We weren't married at the time, but we decided not to rush into anything or get married. We'd just take it one step at a time. In February 1997, we had our healthy baby girl and we were proud parents on cloud nine! She changed our lives in a great way. It's amazing how becoming a parent can change your life and the amount of love that you have for your children. Several months after our daughter was born, we decided to get married, and in November 1998 we got married and moved into our first house. Joe had a great job. He attended college while I stayed at home with our daughter and took a few classes myself.

Life seemed to be great and we were so happy! We enjoyed vacationing and being with our family and friends. We were having a good time with life and in March 2002, we were blessed with another baby girl. How much better could life be?

Well, the following month my husband got laid off. That was quite a journey, and it eventually landed us in another state. We had never moved to another state, as we were born and raised in the one place. He was offered a great job with an aircraft company and we jumped on the chance; however, we were very scared of the unknown! We settled in our new house before the holidays of 2003. Things were great for our family, and we seemed to be living our life to the fullest with our girls!

We were unprepared for what lay in our path. In the beginning of 2006, my husband started having some frequent abdominal pain. We decided it was time for him to go see a doctor and find out what was causing it. At first they couldn't figure out the cause of his pain, so he had to go through several appointments and testing before we received a diagnosis. We were given a diagnosis of lymphoma, a cancer of the lymphocytes that is a part of your immune system. We were in shock, but we were told it was curable and he started chemo treatment immediately. Honestly it just didn't seem to register in my mind; time seemed to fly by between the days when we received a diagnosis to the time he started treatment. I'm not exactly sure what happened next as some of the details are jumbled in my mind. Somewhere along the line, the chemo wasn't working and he ended up getting a biopsy at the end of February 2006. A new doctor gave us a new diagnosis—Ewing's sarcoma. The best I can describe it would be a bone cancer.

Ewing's sarcoma is a type of cancer that is typically seen in children and young adults, so we were referred to a local children's hospital. I will never forget our physician's words. "We are about to go through some rough waters, but I will be here to guide you." I think it was a pretty quiet ride home as it was all just sinking in. What had just happened? Our lives had just taken a major shift. I mean, growing up you heard about cancer, but you just didn't think it could happen to you or grasp the reality of it. Our experience was surreal. I kept thinking I'd wake up and it would just be a dream, but it never happened.

I don't think there was a time that we sat down and really processed everything. We just continued to go through life and didn't allow the cancer to rule us. I was optimistic because Joe was—he had such a positive attitude and outlook. During the chemotherapy, radiation, surgery, clinical trials, and multiple, multiple appointments back to back, we tried to live as normal a life as we could. There were definitely days when Joe did not feel well and it was hard because he was always an active person, but he always tried to be in the best of spirits. I always admired that in him.

There came a point where things didn't look so great and not until years later did a neighbor friend tell me about witnessing a special moment Joe and I had shared. She saw us out in the front yard and I just crawled up into Joe's lap. It was that moment where we both knew things weren't getting any better. I lost my heart in April 2007. I think about it now and at that time, it seemed to go by in slow motion. However, from where I'm at now looking back, it happened so fast, like in the blink of an eye. How did I go from being so happy and enjoying life to where I was at now?

I didn't have a clue what to do with myself, let alone for our family. I was now responsible for our baby girls that needed to be taken care of. I had support around me from family and friends, but I just wanted to be alone. I pushed everyone away. Inside I was so utterly miserable; my world was so dark. I dove into school full time and worked full time, which I disliked so much. All I wanted to do was disappear. I wanted time to stop, I did not want the days to continue, but that never happened.

Time just kept moving on. I ignored what my body was telling me, that I needed to stop and process my feelings, to start healing. I told myself I just had to block that out because I didn't have time to deal with those things. I had to go on day to day, and life didn't stop because I wanted it to. I was trying to figure my own way out of it, which I was lousy at. My stress level increased drastically and my health suffered. I developed high blood

Are you a Christian businesswoman who would like to have the fellowship and support of fellow Christian women entrepreneurs? Visit us at www.nacwe.org to join the fastest growing network of women just like you.

Are you a businesswoman looking for a safe place to connect with fellow sisters of faith who understand the obstacles and challenges you face on a daily basis? Visit www.nacwe.org and discover the rich network of friends and resources that are available to you.

Are you walking through your own Rock Bottom and need some encouragement and support? Visit http://rockbottomisabeautifulplace.com/rock-bottom-gift/and sign up to get our FREE GIFT to you.

pressure, psoriasis, and depression. I couldn't find happiness anywhere. It seemed to elude me.

I felt I wasn't fulfilling my full potential at work and I made a job switch I thought I'd like, only to find myself working more hours and spending less time with my girls. It seemed to be one struggle after another. I traded one thing for another, but I just couldn't win. I couldn't find the happiness that I so missed.

After a few years, I felt I had found some happiness again; I met someone and started dating. After some time, I got remarried and things seemed to be good. Over the next few years, we had two boys. With my health struggles, I had some complications and ended up on bed rest with my third baby. After that pregnancy, I knew I needed to do something about my health because it was not good. I found the Institute of Integrative Nutrition and started changing my health around with my fourth pregnancy.

While my health started changing for the better, my marriage suffered. It took me a long time and a lot of soul-searching to come to the conclusion that I needed to file for a divorce. I've gone through many days and nights trying to figure out why I had to go through all this. It's something I would not wish on an enemy. I've drawn so much strength in God through it all, and I know He has a plan for me.

It's the only thing that has given me comfort pushing through the days. He has a purpose and a plan for my life, and I just have to trust Him. I have grown so much through all of this. If you had asked me ten years ago, I wouldn't have thought that I'd be where I am now. Frankly, it just didn't seem possible.

Did I ever think I'd be sharing my story with others? Absolutely not! But I'm finding my own voice, overcoming fears, and telling people my story! I can say without a doubt I've hit rock bottom, and I didn't think I'd come out on the other side.

Thank God that I have.

Kelly is a single mom to four energetic and beautiful children. She is the owner of Coach Kelly Bell and an independent Beachbody Coach. Her greatest joy is to share her story with widows and busy, stressed moms to inspire and help them achieve their health goals. She knows firsthand the struggles, temptations, and roads that lead to an exhausted and unhealthy life and the joy of conquering them. www.coachkellybell.com

COUNTING MY MANY BLESSINGS!

Karen Lindwall-Bourg

A grateful heart is a beginning of greatness. It is an expression of humility. It is a foundation for the development of such virtues as prayer, faith, courage, contentment, happiness, love, and well-being.

– James E. Faust

I do not innately have a grateful temperament. *Do you? Does being thankful, especially in difficult circumstances, come naturally to you?*

I am a wife and mother, left a widow to raise three children on my own at thirty-five years old. I had to discover what gratefulness entailed the hard way. *Has your heart been so broken that you couldn't even appreciate the blessings?*

I am a successful entrepreneur who made some unwise decisions and who had decided to shut down my ministry instead of restoring it. In rebuilding, I have had to make a concerted effort to be grateful every step of the way. *Have you wanted to give up; have you lost the energy to fight and to give thanks?*

I am a biblical counselor, coach, author, and speaker who struggles every day to fulfill my purpose to glorify God and honor Him in all that I do (Revelation 4:11), and to excel in my calling to work "as unto the Lord" at all times (Colossians 3:23). I have to decide, moment by moment, to model gratefulness for those who come to me, trusting me with their problems and hoping for biblical solutions. *How do you choose daily to be thankful? Would anyone describe you as grateful?*

The Miracles of Counting Our Blessings: The Wonder of Tim

When I started counting my blessings, my whole life turned around.
– Willie Nelson

One Thanksgiving, after our third child was born, my husband, Tim, came to show me his discovery of multiple knots under the skin of his neck. We wasted no time getting to the doctor, then went through all sorts of tests and procedures to pinpoint the source of these growths. As a medical technologist, I was somewhat "in the know" and surrounded by other medical professionals, so I felt like our perspectives and expectations were at least somewhat realistic. Finally, at the beginning of the new year, we visited the doctor's office where we were given a definitive diagnosis of Hodgkin's disease.

Over the next four years, Tim endured surgeries, chemotherapies, radiation treatments, and medications of all kinds. I remember thinking way too often that the things we did to cure him of cancer and to bring him "back to life" seemed very inhumane.

During the last four months of Tim's illness, he lived at Baylor Hospital in Dallas. As the options for treatments dwindled, and as a bone marrow transplant failed to help him, I began to realize I would not be bringing my husband home. For 111 days, our routine was as follows: I worked at the hospital laboratory early in the morning while my father and mother-in-love cared for my children; they visited with Tim while I spent time with my children; then they took my children home to supper and to prepare for bed while I visited with Tim alone. One fateful evening, he began to struggle with headaches, and the next morning, we told each other everything was going to be alright, held hands, and said our last goodbyes.

Where are the miracles in stories as tragic as these? How does a young widow who feels as if her life has been turned upside down and who struggles to breathe enough times to make it through the day express gratitude to the Maker and Taker of Life?

I turned to God in desperation. I knew He was there. Eventually, I could look back and again be grateful this diagnosis was Hodgkin's disease and not another more difficult cancer. Many times, when people came to visit and to help us, they would leave exclaiming that Tim ministered to them more than they helped him. He was always patient, always gracious, always thankful for every care offered to him, and always very loving. I remember his example and try to be like him.

> *I know that I began to really grow in and heal through my grief*
> *and mourning when I was more grateful for the years I had with*
> *Tim than I was sorrowful for the years we weren't going to share.*
> *This was a great and healing turning point for me.*

Like David in the twenty-eighth Psalm, we are able to be thankful in the midst of hard circumstances. We can cry out to God in great distress for His mercy and protection and know that God has heard our cry. He will be our strength and shield, our hearts can still trust in Him and be helped, and we can give thanks to Him in song.

The Vision of the Entrepreneur

There are no mistakes, no coincidences,
all events are blessings given to us to learn from.
– Elisabeth Kubler-Ross

RHEMA Counseling Associates opened our office doors in the summer of 2007, and I naively assumed that because we "built it, they would come!" I knew little about what it took to establish and support a business or ministry of this magnitude. I was still in school (I still am!), was raising a blended family, was helping manage a small farm—I was wearing many hats! I made a lot of decisions along the way that hindered our progress instead of helped it. I wasn't always a good steward of the many things we were offered and missed out on a lot of opportunities. I knew little about establishing boundaries in leading a team of people and therefore, made poor and almost dangerous relationship decisions along the way. At one point, even to the insiders in our alliance, it became difficult to perceive who was actually leading the team and who was following. I had given the key to my heart, my family, and my ministry to another who did not have the same mission and vision I did. By the time I realized boundaries needed to be redefined and reestablished, I felt I would need to take legal action to preserve and protect the organization I had at one time so dearly loved.

Once the dust settled, while I struggled quietly with deciding whether or not to shut down our counseling practice, God placed a vision on my husband Fred's heart, and he appealed to me to consider investing some time and money into rebuilding according to the original dream the Lord had given me. We prayed about it, and soon (about twenty minutes later!) I felt a renewed passion for the work we were called to do!

Where are the miracles in stories of entrepreneurship as complicated as these? How does a new entrepreneur who wants to serve the Lord survive and succeed?

Building an inspired business is like a roller coaster ride for me—one day I am exasperated with technology, or the many details required to define our competitive advantage, or with the feeling that there are not enough hours in my day. The next day I feel like I'm opening Christmas presents, seeing this service organization from new perspectives, and watching families rebuild, marriages renew, and individuals be reborn!

I thank God for the lessons learned and for new direction from a Christian business coach, our lawyer, our prayer partners, and our blessed RHEMA Associates team. From the beginning, I had the support of my husband and my family, my church and pastor, and of those who taught me, and of several who wanted to work alongside me. What a blessing! In my first counseling office experience, I worked with a group of people who supported and taught one another and consistently encouraged a biblical view of life's problems. I knew if I ever had an organization of my own, I would want to follow this supportive pattern. At RHEMA, even in our darkest moments, some of our counselors stood beside me, encouraging and trusting me to do the right thing with this association. And while that sometimes seemed to place an extra burden of great leadership on my shoulders, it has always been a tremendous encouragement to me and given me strength. I owe a lot to and am grateful for these counselors and dear friends! I am grateful!

The Purpose-filled Dream of the Biblical Counselor

Some wish for blessings, others pray for them;
some send blessings, and they become one.
– Joyce C. Lock

Strengths Finder, passion, personality, and temperament tests label me as a helper. My early education was in biology and medical technology, and for eighteen years I absolutely loved the process of providing expedient and accurate medical tests that would help the medical team diagnose and suggest a treatment plan for patients. Along the way, I also thoroughly enjoyed and was fascinated by the social sciences and by theology. There was a time when Tim and I felt we were called to foreign missions. I began to plan in that direction by attending seminary and working toward a degree in counseling. We were newly married and pursuing further education for three years, bearing three stair-step children for the next four years, and then fighting cancers for the next four years of our eleven years of marriage.

Several years later, as a remarried mother of a blending family with my new husband Fred, I finally had an opportunity to return to school and finish my masters in counseling, and then began studying toward a PhD in family therapy. I have always wanted to be able to counsel from a biblical view in a way that consistently pointed people to the Redeemer as the source of all solutions to all problems. I had the great privilege of working with a group of Christian counselors in North Texas that introduced me to biblical counseling.

As soon as I received my first license, I procured a DBA business name, built a website, bought a name tag, and hit the floor running and loving every moment! Okay, *not* running, but crawling at a snail's pace. Alright, *not* loving every moment, but enduring lots of trials! To be a help, to encourage and offer support to those who come to me with their deepest desperations, is one of the most difficult things I have ever attempted to do. I carry my counselees' burdens home with me too often! I get mired down in the details of hundreds of pages of ethical code and responsibilities. In addition, as a follower of Christ, there is a higher standard to uphold (James 3:1 says we will be judged with greater strictness [ESV]). I love America, but we are constantly seeing our freedoms as Christians being challenged and almost every time Christian counselors are in large groups, there will be at least one discussion about an attempt of our government to limit our freedoms to counsel from the Word of God.

An AWANA Clubs teenager once explained to me that we all have the same purpose in life: to make sure God receives glory and honor in everything we do (Revelation 4:11). We all have different callings and are to work heartily, as for the Lord (Colossians 3:23). If I am honest, I must admit I want what I want more often than I want to honor God in all I do. But I at least "want to" want to honor Him. And that's a start!

Where are the miracles for the helper who desires to please the Lord? How does the servant who lives in and works in such changing times remain true and steadfast in this calling?

I vow to keep doing what God has laid on my heart to do, to serve Him as long as I am able—even when I don't feel like it. I cling to every testimony and kind word of every client who is willing to come back to our offices and show us how God has changed their lives. I am so grateful for those who led the way, for those who support and encourage me, and for those who faithfully stayed by my side all the way! I try to remember to celebrate the milestones and not dwell on the pitfalls, especially those I have little control over changing! I am thankful for the current freedoms we have to serve the Lord and to speak openly of Him in our businesses and ministries. I know I am responsible to help promote and protect and preserve those freedoms.

The Surrender of a Grateful Heart

Living in gratitude each day for the gift of a second chance means we:

- focus on God (not on self) and who He is while we consider our circumstances
- ask God to fulfill His promises (2 Samuel 7)
- count our many blessings—every day, we should try to seek the Lord and be reminded that we can choose to focus on the blessings more than on our struggles
- love the Lord, Who is faithful to keep His covenant and love us steadfastly (Deuteronomy 7:9)
- realistically assess and dedicate ourselves to His purpose (to bring Him glory and honor) as we work to fulfill our calling and our vision and dreams
- love and appreciate the team He sends to help us more than we love ourselves (Philippians 28:6-7)!
- speak words of gratitude and appreciation always, sharing the miracles with others.

Like David, after I cry out to God in my distress, I can say:

Blessed be the LORD! For He has heard the voice of my pleas for mercy. The LORD is my strength and my shield; in Him my heart trusts, and I am helped; my heart exults, and with my song I give thanks to Him. (Psalm 28:6-7, ESV)

Again, being grateful does not come naturally to me. It is not part of my "make up." Instead, I more often am the pouty child who desperately needs a Redeemer! And because of God's presence in my life, because of who He is, I am learning to be grateful!

I vow to make that effort every day, moment by moment! How about you!?

Count your blessings instead of your crosses;
Count your gains instead of your losses.
Count your joys instead of your woes;
Count your friends instead of your foes.
Count your smiles instead of your tears;
Count your courage instead of your fears.
Count your full years instead of your lean;
Count your kind deeds instead of your mean.
Count your health instead of your wealth;
Count on God instead of yourself.
– Author Unknown

Karen Lindwall-Bourg is the founder of RHEMA Counseling Associates, a biblical counseling, coaching, and training center that seeks to honor the Lord by leading others to the Sovereign God, the cross and life of Jesus Christ, empowerment by the Holy Spirit, and equipped with the Sufficient Word [Greek: rhema] of God for abundant life and ministry. Karen lives with her husband, Fred, in north central Texas and spends as much time as possible with their six children, five grandchildren, extended family, and a menagerie of ranch animals. You can find out more about RHEMA Counseling Associates at www.rhemacounseling.com.

A LEGACY CHANGED

Shannon Bowman

What seems to us as bitter trials are often blessings in disguise.

– Oscar Wilde

When pondering upon what I would share with you, I began to recount times in my life of hopelessness and despair. I wondered if any of these instances were worth writing about and was concerned that my story did not have the "weight" of others, that people would judge my story as trivial.

I struggle with my worth. Insecurity plagues me. Wrong beliefs whisper and repeat in my mind. Every single day is a battle, and some battles have laid me out for longer than I would like to admit. It starts with overanalyzing, which leads to fear and freaking out. Then I hide, which leads to paralysis. The past few years I have been hiding under a bush and not letting my light shine, and that light was almost extinguished.

Struggling with what to say and where to begin, I saw a picture of myself standing on a pile of rocks at the bottom of a pond. My feet were submerged in water, and I realized that the water was draining slowly out from underneath me. Soon it would be dried up. The life was leaking out. It was an accurate illustration of what had been happening to me over the last couple of years.

Sometimes we hit rock bottom because we have been drained. Sucked dry. The burdens and obligations of everyday life can be overwhelming. Being a mom to three boys and homeschooling is a wonderful blessing, but it is hard. We have autism spectrum challenges and sensory issues which make things difficult. Family does not live close by, and my husband travels quite a bit due to work. No support in a rural area where you are not embraced readily because your roots don't run deep. Trying to make it all work and adjust to a different life, and just when it seems that things are on track, BAM! You are hit by the freight train that you had seen coming in the distance, but could not predict its arrival. This train happened to be my grandmother's situation.

I call her Grandmommie, and she is a charming, fun, and witty lady. Everyone loves her, and she never meets a stranger. There are such fond memories of making marzipan, painting ceramics, and shopping trips. If it was purple, which I happen to still adore, she would buy it for me. I was introduced to garage sales and thrift stores through her, and my "hope chest" was a constant conversation. She poured out her love with baubles and trinkets, but it was also the bane of our relationship. The way I like to describe it is that she was a "keeper," meaning she kept just about everything and was constantly buying things for herself and others that were not needed.

I have memories of sleeping in a bed surrounded by boxes from floor to ceiling when I would spend the night at her house. It was always like this, so I didn't know any different. As the years went by, the rest of the house started to fill up, and I would hear her mention storage rooms. I lived with her for a few months during college, thinking I could maybe help her in some way, but I was always met with resistance when I tried to do anything.

Years later, I found myself in a place where I had to take action. Nothing could have prepared me for what I was about to engage in, yet God had been getting me ready for months. I did not want to deal with any of it; it was too painful. There were other people involved who did not like my decisions, and I felt tormented and helpless. When I laid it all down and surrendered to God, He made a way. It was quite miraculous. Strangers came out of nowhere to help, and we had a prayer meeting together in the midst of a horrific mess.

I found gifts bought for me as a child that I never received. Wrapping paper with my name printed in rainbow colors, and a set of purple ponytail holders brought me a smile in the midst of despair. A vast collection of clothes from years past had been ruined by mold and mildew, other clothes were donated, and I was told not to bring anymore. The amount of items was unfathomable. It was tragic proof of years of suffering. We all cope with hurt in various ways, and we build walls to protect our wounded hearts. You could actually see her walls and it was overwhelming. Grandmommie had been hiding behind all of this mess. She was a hurt, wounded little girl inside, just like I was.

Many months later, my concern increased, and I was compelled to look at other houses in our area to accommodate her. As we lived in the country, that proved to be cumbersome, but the Lord was directing my steps and He led us to the "hummingbird house." As soon as I walked in the door, I thought of my grandmother because of the hummingbirds on the wallpaper. She adored animals in general, but had an affinity for hummingbirds. This was on a Thursday, and I was leaving the next day to help with a women's retreat. Since I would be only an hour away from where she was living, my plan was to go by and visit her on Monday. Expecting to just take her shopping, I found myself in a place of making a difficult choice that would adversely affect people that I loved. She was in a situation that was perilous and called for drastic measures. I called my husband to tell him that I was going to be bringing her home. He made an offer on the hummingbird house, and we had a contract on it on Thursday. In just a matter of a week, the Lord had delivered my grandmother as well as a place to care for her in.

So I brought my grandmother to my tiny home in the country to figure out how I was going to handle it all. We were fine for a few weeks, but then she wanted to go home. She did not want to move into the beautiful home where a lovely room was waiting for her. I will never forget the night that a police car showed up in our driveway because she was adamant about going home and had gone to the neighbor's house in the middle of the night. My autism training began to come into use as I dealt with a special needs child in an adult body.

I injured my back at some point before we moved, and this made things more complicated. The Lord used all of this to reiterate to me Psalm 121:2: "My help comes from the Lord, the Maker of heaven and earth" (NIV). I really didn't want to hear it because I wanted something tangible. The doubt was palpable, and though I never lost of my faith, I began to lose myself.

We moved and because everyone had their own space, things were more manageable. A place to retreat from the strange behaviors, requests, and conversations she would exhibit. She began to grow increasingly irritated and mean to us. It was confusing for my children, and we took the opportunities to talk about grace and love, and what Jesus had done for us. That her brain was hurt, and she couldn't help it. Schooling was interrupted constantly, she was never content, and she created problems when she could not get attention.

I longed for it to be different, that we would live together as one happy family, but I knew that it was not going to last. Eventually, I made the heart-wrenching decision to move Grandmommie to a place where she would be cared for and be close to other family members. It grieved my heart because I felt like a failure. I did not want strangers watching over her, comforting her. I wanted more time.

In the midst of exhaustion and chaos, there were precious moments I had with her that I am so grateful for. We had wonderful times of laughter and snuggling and watching *The Lawrence Welk Show*. Looking at pictures and reminiscing of the fun we had together when I was a child. She would always thank me for bathing her, even though she fought it every step of the way.

I will not presume to tell you what God was doing with it all, because I know that is beyond my reach. I thought things would be on an upswing after I moved her. We would return to a family of five, establish a new routine, and move on with life. However, that was not the case. Betrayal happened in several different directions with people I loved and trusted. People that our family had poured love and life into had sideswiped me, and I was devastated. I love deep, and I am also wounded deep. Then I had a simple outpatient procedure and had an allergic reaction to the anesthesia. I thought I was going to die. The pond had but a trickle of water left, and I questioned the purpose of anything and everything.

As humans, we can't help but have judgements about the exterior of another person. It is part of our nature. Someone who is fun to be around, loves to laugh, and looks pulled together is still carrying heavy burdens. And nobody will ask. Because they are afraid themselves. Aren't we all? To say the wrong thing, or to not want to be transparent and vulnerable. Uncomfortable. Just trying to keep it altogether. I had the keys to unlock the bondage I was in, but I was too tired to use them.

The truth I was ashamed of and the lies that I believed kept me in a place where I leaked life.

Screaming at the bottom of a pond, on top of a pile of rocks, and nobody will come throw me a lifeline. Rock bottom. So painful, yet a most beautiful place because Jesus was there. He watched me and waited while I threw my fits and cried. He held me when I slept and gently pushed me out of bed when I had convinced myself that I couldn't do it anymore. I don't know when it happened, but many months later, I was different. It's like this stagnant part of me had been revitalized, reactivated. I had never stopped talking or holding onto Him, and He was faithful. It had just taken awhile to heal, to plug up all the holes that I had been leaking out of.

Being grateful is emphasized greatly in our house, and it is something I want to impart to my children. To take joy in all things, no matter how awful they are. There are mysteries that we will never understand, but we carry on and remain thankful and count our blessings. I am humbled that I was given the chance to see my grandmother through God's eyes. I was able to love on the little girl inside of her, inside of me, and change my thoughts on the legacy that she left me. Forgiveness took on a new meaning and was empowering. My strength is undeniable, and I am not afraid to shine my light anymore.

Shannon Bowman is a homeschool mom to three boys and resides in southwest Missouri. She is passionate about purple, collects teacups, is an avid thrift store shopper, and can't have enough books or animals. Event planning, etiquette classes, and organizational services are a few of her business activities, and she is pursuing a PhD in Spiritual Health and Healing. Her heart is set on helping people see themselves through God's eyes, and to give special needs children a voice by encouraging their parents. Shannon would love to connect with you at www.shanbowman.com.

COMMUNITY HURTS AND COMMUNITY HEALS

Elizabeth Buhrke

I will offer You my grateful heart, for I am Your unique creation, filled with wonder and awe. You have approached even the smallest details with excellence; Your works are wonderful; I carry this knowledge deep within my soul.

– Psalm 139:14 (VOICE)

I know that rock bottom is a beautiful place because it has been in many of those rock bottom places that I have found purpose to keep on living! There have been countless times where I have found previous hardship, trauma, or chaos of life bring meaning to my life and the lives of those around me. The fact that you are reading this is evidence that God is shining through the broken pieces of my life to encourage or strengthen others.

I watched a movie this weekend about a young Muslim boy who went to public school and was bullied, so his father moved him to a private Muslim boarding school where he ended up being beaten. The result was that he questioned his Muslim faith. It was through a series of events around 9/11, while he was in college, where the secret he was carrying of these beatings came out to his family and his real healing began. That healing began with forgiveness.

Forgiveness is where my healing grows deeper and where my gratefulness stems. My story has many similarities to this young man's and has led ME to question my Christian faith on numerous occasions. My life is still affected by the years of sexual abuse I endured in a small rural Christian day school attached to the church my father pastored. I often think about how the boys that were one to three years older than me are probably living their lives with no thoughts about our lives in grade school together, while I still struggle to trust and let anyone in close enough to see my internal scars.

BUT GOD...but God has moved in my heart to be friends with some of their family members on Facebook and even one of them. But God... allowed me to visit this school a few years ago and walk the hallway with my own son to show him where I went to school when I was his age, and even stand in the doorway to the classroom where it all occurred. I don't find it ironic at all that after all of the renovations that have occurred to add additional space to this school building, this particular classroom remains fairly unchanged all these years later.

While my path to healing has been bumpy, leading me down a destructive path filled with addictions and rebellion and other dangerous behaviors, God's hand has been on me. I've spent way too many years being angry with God for having let bad things happen to me, only to come to an understanding that His heart broke with every vile incident I endured and every bad choice I made because of them.

I almost died a couple of times from eating disorders, but He saved my life. Doctors could not explain how on earth my internal organs had not shut down during my last semester of college. That is how I know it was God. There was no science that could make sense of why I was still alive and functioning. A few years before that, I couldn't explain how I survived a brutal rape my first year in college or getting out of a gang. A couple of months after getting out of the hospital, I couldn't explain how my life would be changed forever by becoming pregnant.

God spared my life that cold December night my first year of college. I went through a decision-making process about whether to abort, carry and raise my child myself, or carry and give up my child for adoption that would become essential a few years later when I would become pregnant with my son. It is because of the process of questioning I had previously gone through my freshman year of college that my son is even here today. All a part of God's plan from the very beginning, but definitely a process I've had to work through to get to where I am today.

The AMAZING thing about this journey of faith that I've been on is that while at times I have felt entirely alone, the fact of the matter is, God has brought people into my life during specific seasons of this journey that have been integral to my healing process. For so many years, I questioned my private Christian day school upbringing because I couldn't make sense out of learning about this loving God one minute in religion class and then questioning how a loving God would allow these horrific things I endured. It wasn't until I became a parent and saw that my son at that young age did not have the vocabulary to explain things like that if they would've happened to him, so why should I continue to beat myself up for not telling someone sooner about those events years ago? This was one of my first steps in forgiving myself. (Please do not read this wrong...in NO WAY was I to blame for my innocence being taken away from me, but the actions, choices, and decisions I made out of those places of pain have required my attention and forgiveness throughout this process.)

Yet it has been this education that has allowed me the biblical knowledge and love for God's Word to teach others about God's Word in Bible studies and conferences/retreats today. It has also been this education that has given me the wisdom and understanding necessary to walk into the healing God has for me. Although my healing that makes me whole in God's eyes was completed on the cross over 2000 years ago, I find this journey a process toward that wholeness that is only possible in Him.

There are countless people who have been a part of this healing journey that I'm grateful beyond words for. Some of them know who they are, while others may never know how they have impacted my life. There are people I've walked and done life with who have known some of my struggles, and others I've walked with that have shared life with me never knowing that their presence was exactly what I needed exactly then.

Those high school teachers who kept in contact with me after moving a state away showed their investment in me was more than just in the classroom. There was a college professor my last semester of college who reached out to me when she saw signs that were concerning to her. Even though I lied to her and explained things away to lead her to believe that I was okay, her concern gave me some much needed encouragement and reminded me that I wasn't alone. There was an entire church body that wrapped their loving arms around me to show me what Christ's unconditional love was as a young mother struggling to make ends meet. They loved me in a way that was necessary for me to learn to love myself.

I remember my dear friend sitting across the table from me as we shared a meal during a time I was struggling with my eating, and had the patience to sit with me for hours just so I could finish a small fruit cup. Another friend welcomed me into her life, at times putting her family on hold to spend time with me even when she may not have wanted to. And then there are ALL of those friends who have made me laugh along the way. If I've laughed with you, you have had an impact on my life.

What about the women's ministry team who helped me find my strengths and showed me how I could use my God-given talents to glorify His name? That same church body that showed me I am loved allowed me to spread my wings both within their walls and by letting me move on, all while welcoming my son and me back, much like we do as family when our children grow up and move out. We are welcomed back on visits, and loved and encouraged in each moment we are together. A godmother who connected with me at a young age and remained engaged, supported me along the way by allowing me to tell her anything. Who would have known that after receiving a gift from her (probably thirty-five years ago), that it would be an integral part of my healing journey today? God knew!

The special note of a grandfather who ALWAYS signed any correspondence to me "God loves you and so do I" that I held onto in some of my darkest moments and missed the most after he went to be with Jesus. And last but not least, parents who have loved me the best way they've known how through all of it. While I know they will be the first to say they have not gotten it all right (I only share this because I've heard my mother say it on more than one occasion), they raised me to know God, allowing Him to fill in the missing pieces where they may have come up short or messed up. I did not get to where I am today on my own. It has taken more patience than I can imagine. It has been the faith of those around me along this journey that has been a witness to me in my life and encouraged me to hang on all of those times I've just wanted to give up. Many times it's been the faith of others that has carried me until I was able to grow in my own relationship with Jesus.

It's been that faith of those around me that's carried me through when I had it with God. I know it's taken praying grandparents, parents, extended family, and friends throughout the years. It's those examples that have been so important in getting me to this place in my life and that I strive for in my own life now as I venture out on this journey of faith towards a deeper understanding of the unconditional love of this God whom I serve. It's been through the forgiveness of those who have intentionally harmed me, along with forgiveness of those I expected to protect me from that harm, and finally the forgiveness of myself for the choices and decisions and actions I took from that place of hurt I lived in for way too long.

I'm not ALWAYS grateful for the path I've taken on this journey, if I can be totally honest with you, but as I dare to live a life after God, that gratefulness grows day by day. It's been through my rock bottom places where God has met me, sometimes through people that were my Jesus with skin on, that allows me to live with a grateful heart even in and amongst my brokenness. The people that God has placed along my path and the experiences through which He has walked with me have helped mold me into the best mother I am able to be for my son, the best friend I know how to be (even in my failing at it miserably sometimes), and the best woman I know how to be, reaching after God.

I'm grateful for not always getting things right because it has been in those areas I have fallen short that I have grown the most in my love for God and those around me. It's been in the struggles of life that I find my courage to keep facing those fears and challenging myself to a deeper wholeness in this God that I love.

Elizabeth Buhrke is a worship leader at heart. She has just recently returned to speaking and sharing what God has done in her life after a ten-year hiatus. Elizabeth's passion for the Lord compels her to share, through word and song, the dark places from which Christ has drawn her. Her foundational joy is rooted in Christ and reflected brightly in the life of her son. She counts them both as integral reasons she is alive and empowered to share the gospel with others today.

THE DAY MY WORLD TURNED UPSIDE DOWN

Annette Filmer Dean

Our deepest fear is not that we are inadequate. Our deepest fear is that we are powerful beyond measure. It is our light, not our darkness, that most frightens us...And as we let our light shine, we unconsciously give other people permission to do the same. As we are liberated from our own fears, our presence automatically liberates others.

– Marianne Williamson, *Return to Love*

As I sat there on our brand new computer, I was trying to figure out how all these emails came to my inbox. I didn't recognize the addresses; however, we were just learning how to operate this new PC. It was the time when multiple laptops, iPods, iPhones, desktops, and smart TVs were not yet part of the standard furniture in everyone's home. We were just embarking on this thing, and I still hadn't wrapped my brain around the fact that you could send an instant message, let alone email. Who were these emails from? I sat, confused, as I opened them up. I began to read the contents of one of the emails, and my stomach tightened. The more I read, the more the confusing thoughts swirled in my head and the shock began to take hold of my body.

My thoughts raced. Who was this woman that wrote these emails? Was my husband cheating on me? How did his email account come up instead of mine? Was this some sick, twisted joke? Why was she even saying these inappropriate things!? What in God's name was going on?

My chest tightened and I thought my heart would just explode. My face flushed as a shock wave coursed through me like nothing I had experienced before. My whole world as I knew it began to fall apart. I was in complete disbelief, horrified, trying to fit the puzzle pieces together, sorting, scrambling, and catching my breath.

How? Why? Who? When? This was NOT happening! As I mustered up the courage to read through the rest of the details, I realized these were facts. There was no mistaking the information was accurate because she would never have known what she did if she hadn't had an affair with my husband. No question. I knew in this very moment that my entire life had just shattered...forever.

Devastated, I tried desperately to hold on to any sort of rational reasoning that I could. What should I do? I couldn't talk to my family—they would be so hurt and devastated. I needed to call my best friend. I needed to take my daughter and get out of there. I needed to leave this house and life that had all been built on a façade of lies!! All lies!! Where did the truth end and the lies begin?

My baby girl...how could he do this to us? He had destroyed us, our reputation, our life, our whole family, friends, church leadership...

everything! From then on, everything unraveled. Hour by hour, day by day, week by week, story upon story of the unthinkable. Multiple affairs, webs of lies, the so-called friends, the jobs he was fired from when I was led to believe he quit. The side jobs, the trips to the store, the "I got talking to so and so" excuses, the late nights out on the town...all began to form the bigger picture of the puzzle of our fabricated life.

Welcome. I am Annette, and this is my rock bottom.

There was not a bone in my body on that earth-shattering day that could imagine this would one day possibly be one of my biggest life blessings. I want to tell you today I have clear twenty-twenty hindsight, understanding, and a compassion forged from the flames of my rock bottom that helps me to help others who find themselves walking through the fires of desperation. It slowly, gradually became a beautiful place from which I would find a deeper love, a more genuine unconditional love I may not have paid much attention to otherwise. It began the difficult tearing down and destruction necessary to rebuild my spiritual and emotional solid foundation, the one that began as the beautiful, rocky road that led me down the path of my destiny to my most authentic, genuine, highest self.

Beyond a shadow of a doubt, God got my attention that day. He had a plan that I had ZERO idea about. Little did I know where it would lead me to and through, what it would deliver me out of. I never would have had my heart healed the way my Creator and Designer has healed it. You don't just jump on the crazy train and say to God, "HEY!!... Come on, God!! Please let my heart get smashed into zillions of pieces until it is unrecognizable and I cannot possibly put the pieces back together by myself, so you can heal it perfectly! Let's do this!"

No, we avoid pain at all costs. It's counterintuitive. This time, I couldn't avoid it, however. My eyes were opened wide to the ugly truth of what my life was secretly made of. I want to say I had no choice, but that is not the truth. I had choices, just not any great ones. It was a choice of the lesser of the evils, the least damaging over time. I had to get out and let God restore me so that I would be able to give my daughter and any future children a healthy legacy.

It tore my heart out for so many reasons. I never wanted to be a single mom, divorced, alone, the bread winner and provider while raising my baby. However, the reality was that having this precious baby girl's life to consider empowered me to make the difficult choices that would be healthier for both of us. We tend to remain the same, until the pain of remaining the same is greater than the pain of change itself. The pain of remaining, for me, was now unbearable. Change was inevitable.

The next day, I sat home alone on what I thought was our once beautiful consecrated bed, sobbing, unable to see the words of my rather unused Bible in front of me. I had not confronted him yet. He didn't know I knew anything at all. I needed time, a few days to get some sort of rational strategy together. I was never so afraid or lost in my entire life. Questions still raced in my mind day after day and night after night. I began to see him as a stranger in my house, someone who masqueraded as my closest confidant, best friend, cherished lover, and brave protector of our precious little growing family.

BOOM! Massive brain disconnect. I cried out to God, who, by the way, I had previously kept in a nice, neat, perfect religious box, tied up with a pretty bow for quite some time now. He was there to pray to sometimes, ask for things from, and now, to beg and plead with, as I wanted Him to make this living nightmare disappear.

"Please take this lot from me, God! Why ME??" In my limited understanding, He was a strict, often condemning, parental figure who was generally angry, waiting to inflict punishment and guilt with every little mistake or sin I committed. Not exactly the loving, giving, Designer of my very soul that I now know Him to be, the One who has orchestrated every single miniscule event of my life—the good, the bad, and yes, even the ugly. Religious legalism will kill your spirit, squelch your ability to live within the purest space of love and deepest compassion for others, and possibly leave you squirming as one frustrated, critically judgmental individual who has theories and rules that demand everyone else fit into them. It's a one-size-fits-all and we protect this concept at all costs because the thought of anything else means self-reflection. It reveals the need to shred the ego, the pride, and the arrogance of self-righteousness that comes along with it, and yes, they all hang out together. It was a tough pill to swallow. The tearing down had now begun.

As I was sitting there, grieving deeply, heartbroken, afraid, alone, confused, and angry, the tears pouring continuously with no end in sight, I saw something in my mind's eye, my spirit. I didn't even know or understand at that time in my life that it was actually a vision from God Himself. This vision would serve me many times over as He brought it to my remembrance while I carried on with life far beyond those pits of despair. He was in the process of allowing destruction through the revealing of truth to take place in this season. You see, you cannot rebuild a strong, secure foundation until you have torn down and destroyed the old model, the old patterns, the defective structure. Only then can you replace them with new, healthier, happier patterns that serve the highest purposes for your life. He began to show me this.

In this vision, I was standing upright on a flat concrete floor. A large, smooth slab extended out from under my feet for as far as my eyes could see. There was nothing around me, nothing on the ground, nothing in the atmosphere. It was just as dark as the midnight sky. Blackness surrounded me just beyond the extension of my arm's reach. I stood, unable to move my feet in any direction, and with the instinctual urge to remain with my feet firmly planted.

As I looked into the distance, I began to see something in the concrete. I squinted my eyes, straining to see what looked like a tiny hairline crack forming in the concrete. The crack would creep out a little bit at a time. Each time it would become not only longer, but wider and wider, deeper and deeper as it made its way closer to me. I quickly whirled my head around to look behind me, only to discover the same thing was happening there. I looked frantically from one side, then to the other, realizing this entire concrete slab that appeared to be so secure and solid was falling apart! I panicked! As the cracks grew closer toward me and pieces began to crumble, huge chunks of a once solid floor just fell away into a void of darkness. Fear gripped my heart as the urge to hold on to something, ANYTHING, coursed through me.

I need to hold steady, I thought. I needed to hold on for balance. I longed for an anchor to keep me from falling, yet, nothing was around me to save me. Natural instincts urge you to grab hold and latch onto something sturdy, steady, unmovable. However, there was nothing to be found. It was in this moment that I realized God was removing all the "props" I had relied on in my life up until now. Those props weren't intrinsically bad things, they were just crutches that I had unknowingly used in my efforts to help myself through life. We all do it. It's a natural behavior. We cling to the things that bring us some sort of comfort, routine, or seem safe and secure.

It may be material possessions, codependent relationships, our own children even, never-ending counseling, drugs, alcohol, marijuana, status and prestige in the public eye. All these things can hinder our truest, strongest core security, which is the Creator Himself. That day, He loved me enough to show me that He was all I would ever need for a lifetime of security, counsel, and hope. He wanted me to fully trust Him to lead me, teach me, and to have my back. He wanted to satisfy the longings of my heart and be my first true love. Only then would He be able to use me to love others the way He had done for me.

I thought for sure I would drop into an abyss of darkness and unknown territory. Then I heard the words, "Look up. Just reach up." *Huh?* I thought, but there was nothing tangible above me. Desperate for safety and a sense of security, I stretched my arms straight up, like a young child reaching up to her loving father to pick her up. Hands straight up in the air, I was steady, unusually balanced, and with a knowing inside of me that I had never experienced before that I would be alright.

I didn't understand it fully at the time, but I knew deep within my spirit that was where my help would now come from. God has since reminded me of the verse, "When the righteous cry for help, the Lord hears, and delivers them out of all their distresses and troubles. The Lord is close to those who are brokenhearted and saves such as are crushed with sorrow for sin and are humbly and thoroughly penitent" (Psalm 34:17-18 AMP). As I reached up, as massive hunks of thick concrete just fell away piece by piece, it all disappeared right up to where my feet were firmly planted, about an inch or so surrounding the length and width of my feet. It was enough to get the sense it was sturdy, yet not one inch more than I needed, the bare minimum with no room to move or take even one baby step.

Hands held up high, I leaned slightly forward as I peered below this small concrete square that remained under my feet. I saw that it was a pedestal column upon which I remained. It was strong, and I knew in my innermost being that it was solid, steady, unshakable, secure, and immune to destruction of any kind.

It was then that He showed me that He was my pillar of strength, my strong tower, my ever present help in time of need. I never understood it in this way before. He was revealing Himself to me that day in an extraordinary way because He knew I needed Him more than I knew myself. It was here that my rock bottom became what I now can claim as a beautiful place. What kind of a God takes time to speak to little old me like that?? The God of all the universe, that's who. The God who formed me in my mother's womb. The One who knows all my intricacies, right down to the number of hairs on my head. The One who knows the end from the beginning. The One who rescued me and rescues all who will simply cry out to Him. The One who answers our prayers and loves us enough not to leave us desperate in our mess, guiding us out of darkness into His loving light, love, wisdom, and presence. Giving us a beautiful message from our nasty mess to share with others who need to know they are loved by an ever-loving God who created them with a purpose in mind.

That day, the beginning of the "destroy and rebuild" of my life's foundation launched me into a whole new journey of self-loving care, the shredding of man-made religious rules, and the freedom from bondages that had gripped my life, my soul, my identity, and my authentic self. God had more for me, so much more.

Don't get me wrong, it wasn't easy at all. Several years following that day entailed mostly an uphill climb in every area of my life. I learned how to nurture my broken heart, deal with massively difficult, gut-wrenching struggles, break down a façade of smothering, constrictive false beliefs that were not of God, all the while, awakening to His truth for my true identity as His own, and the truth about my life purposes and my legacy. That shocking day of "horror," when I felt like the rug was being pulled out from under me and I was left floundering and lost was the best, most liberating thing that could have ever happened to me. I'm free indeed.

Annette Filmer Dean is a woman of extraordinary courage, faith, and conviction for total wellness. Suffering devastating health challenges, she sought answers, researched, traveled, and invested countless hours and tens of thousands of dollars into her education and recovery. Her discoveries have not only enabled her to take steps toward her own health recovery, but also help hundreds of others through private phone coaching, tele-classes, and weekly blogs. She has been rebuilding every area of her life once again over the past several years, and is looking forward to discovering what the next chapter of her life holds as she leads, encourages, and advocates for others along the journey of healing and wellness. Find out more about Annette here: www.annetteshealingjourney.com or on Facebook: Annette's Healing Journey

WHOM THEN SHALL I FEAR?

Dixie Sims Dobbins

Put on the whole armor of God, that ye may be able to stand against the wiles of the devil. For we wrestle not against flesh and blood, but against principalities, against powers, against the rulers of the darkness of this world, against spiritual wickedness in high places.

– Ephesians 6:11 (KJV)

It was 3 a.m. on a cool April night as I sat in the hot tub with my friend, Allison. The other college students mingled and chatted around the lux condo pool and our Jacuzzi tub. I was not drinking any alcohol, as I was the designated driver.

I decided to get out of the hot tub and walk to my friend's car to get some change for the soft drink machine. I climbed out, dried myself off, and walked alone to the parking lot. After getting the money, I noticed a male figure coming towards me as I turned to walk back to the pool.

I got a strange feeling in my gut and then quickly shirked it off. I told myself, *He's just walking and has every right to be here as I do.* I started for the pool.

Suddenly, without warning, someone grabbed me from behind, put his hand over my mouth, and whispered in my ear, "Where do you stay?" I looked down and saw a flash of silver, and immediately thought it was a gun!

"Answer me!" he growled. "Do you like life? Do what I say and maybe you'll have one." He forced me into the car through the passenger door and made me crawl into the driver's seat. My heart was racing and a thought crossed my mind. *It's my mother's birthday. I'm going to be murdered on my mother's birthday.*

⚜

I had moved to Lubbock, Texas after finally ending a five-year relationship with a man who thought my face and body were his punching bag. I had had enough, and made plans to take a year to attend Texas Tech. I allowed my daughter to live with my ex and his family. I was very sad to leave my little girl as she was only seven. She cried when I decided to take this big step and I cried too, but knew I had to get serious about school, my future, and my safety or I'd forever be stuck as a waitress. I was tired of living week to week on measly tips.

I had divorced her father after his verbal abuse and drinking, and then fell into another abusive relationship. I thought I had found a good man, and it wasn't just a few months before he smashed my face into a clothes hamper for losing his car keys. After five years I finally got the courage to call the police on him after he hit me in the thigh and then hit me in the back with my remote control after I had explained I had to study for a photography test instead of doing his laundry for him. The police acted as if I had made up the story, and I knew I had to get far away from him.

I was working as a cocktail waitress in Lubbock in a popular student nightclub, barely able to pay my bills. My dream was to become a photographer and I could only afford two classes per semester. I had gone out after work with a co-worker that night to blow off some steam and relax when we were invited to the party. I was doing my best to get my life back on track.

❧

"Turn at the light," the stranger said to me, jolting me back to the present. "Now speed up and go to the next light."

I was shaking, following his commands. I thought about crashing the car into another car, but only saw one car in the wee hours of 3:30 a.m. and I missed my one chance. He told me to pull up and stop. On our right was a big pasture with some new homes off about 100 yards away. On the left was a giant caliche pit, a place where rainwater would run and often fill up to the top, but I knew it was empty. I knew where we were.

"Turn off the car," he said, and I obeyed.

"Take off your swimsuit," he demanded.

I hesitated, trembling. "Please..."

"Shut up and stop looking at me. You're just trying to identify me." He looked about twenty years old, African-American, and built like a football player. His eyes were small and slanted, as if he might have been part Asian. I could see the scars on his shoulders, stretch marks from his muscles growing so fast. I thought of my daughter and mother and how devastated they would be when the police told them about finding my body. Eerily, I seemed almost resigned to the fact that I was not going to get out of this alive.

My whole body shook as I sat in the cold leather car seat and I decided to tell him about my daughter. "I-I-I have a little girl," I stammered. "Her name is Misty. I'm all she has."

"Take off your bottoms," he commanded, not hearing anything I was saying. The next few minutes were a blur. Within a minute or so of pulling me over to him on the passenger side, he opened the car door, said it was too crowded in the car, and ordered me to get out. I felt the cold air blow into the car and I pleaded for us to stay inside.

"Step out now!"

I began to step out, knowing what he had in mind. I could see down between his seat and the door, and I saw his hand slide down under the seat, pulling out a large butcher knife. Adrenaline surged through me, and I took off running as fast as I could! I had run track in high school and now I ran like a race horse! I ran with everything I had.

I could hear my feet slapping my bottom as I ran for the houses I saw about a football field away. Then I heard another sound—his feet pounding the ground— and I knew he was right behind me. I found a burst of energy and threw everything into my stride!

Then I felt his hands grabbing my thighs, and everything began happening in slow motion. We were headed for the rocky desert soil, and as I was falling, it seemed that my life flashed before my eyes. I saw my body lying at the bottom of the caliche pit, face down, nude and bloody. I saw my mother's and daughter's faces at my funeral, tears streaming.

Then I thought to myself, *Just because a person gets stabbed, it doesn't mean they always die.*

I could feel his fury behind me, like a heat blast of anger. As we were falling, my horror and terror turned into peace. I felt as if a large container of warm water was pouring all over my body, relaxing me and giving me comfort. For several seconds or so it seemed, I felt safe, warm, and protected.

Then suddenly, I snapped back to reality. I realized that he and I were still sliding across the damp weeds and my fear returned. I was enveloped by pure horror! I told myself that this was it—it was over. Then I heard a Voice saying, "Don't worry, you are not going to die today."

At the same time, I was aware of a light behind us and to our left. I felt as if the Voice had come from that direction. I said to myself, *Yes I am going to die.* That Voice responded in the most reassuring way.

"I *won't* let you die."

A peace surrounded me again, and we finally came to a sliding stop. I stood up and calmly turned towards my attacker. I felt as if I had a suit of armor on me. Surprised, he stood up too, and I blurted, "What happened to you?"

His small eyes widened, and he backed away from me, the knife still grasped in his hand. He appeared to be afraid of me. He said, "I'll tell you what happened to me, if you'll come back to the car with me. I'll tell you everything."

I still felt as if I had on a suit of armor and I knew he could not hurt me. I cannot explain it, I just knew. We sat in the car and he placed the knife back under his seat. He began talking.

"My name is Lawrence Wayne Buford. I'm twenty years old and I'm from California. I moved here because I had been in a gang and got into trouble. I live with my uncle, who's a pharmacist at the Eckerd drug store just over there," he explained, pointing his finger.

He went on and on like a child. He talked until the sun started coming up. Then oddly, he asked me if I was hungry, and I let him drive. We changed seats and he moved the rearview mirror, placing a perfect right thumb print on the glass. *Bingo,* I thought. *Evidence.*

He drove through Burger King. I could tell he knew the girl that worked there and I knew we were on camera. *More evidence,* I thought. A part of me felt sorry for him, and part of me knew he was definitely dangerous. I knew I had to report it.

He drove back to the condos, and then he asked to see my driver's license. I did not want to show him, but he insisted. I showed him and he saw my address, name, and birthdate. Then he said, "Oh no, you're not going to like me anymore."

I played along. "Why?"

"I'm a lot younger than you are," he said, and he got out and walked away. I sat there until he rounded the corner of the building before I jumped over to the driver's seat and drove like a maniac towards my home. I flagged down a policeman and asked him to follow me, as I wanted to report a crime.

After going to the hospital and being interviewed, the police called me a couple of days later and had me pick him out of nine Polaroid photographs lying on a table. I quickly picked him out. My roommates said they saw the police remove a large knife and a pair of thick rubber gloves from the car.

Then the police told me that according to their opinion, I had been a willing participant and had not been kidnapped! I was speechless, and they assured me they were keeping a close eye on him.

I was very ill for the next two weeks. I could not work or eat, and I slept almost all day and night. I was so weak, I had to crawl on my hands and knees to go to the bathroom, and I had to wear sunglasses because light was unbearable. I lived on water and orange juice.

Finally, after twelve days, I was able to eat again and walk around. I decided to attend church that following Sunday and was very weak, but I wanted to be in a house of worship. I sat alone in the back of the church, and the pastor began his sermon with Ephesians 6:11. "Put on the whole armor of God, so that you may stand to the wiles of the devil" (KJ2000). I immediately began sobbing. Hadn't I felt as if I had on a suit of armor as I stood naked, facing that knife-wielding man? Had the Holy Spirit covered me? What was the Voice that said, "I won't let you die?" What was that warmth and peace that surpassed all understanding? Why did he back away from me, fear in his widened eyes? What was that light shining behind me?

I returned to work the next day, and my boss knew what had happened to me. He brought me into his office and seemed very concerned about me. My friend, Allison (who also worked there), had told him what happened to me, and he knew I had needed those two weeks off. I thought he was going to ask me if I was ready to return or needed more time off. He leaned over his desk, his kind blue eyes somber, and asked, "Have you seen today's newspaper?" I shook my head. He opened his desk drawer and pulled it out, laying it in front of me.

The headline read, "Lubbock Woman Beaten, Raped and Stabbed in Critical Care." I began to read the front-page article about a twenty-four-year-old woman who was in ICU, fighting for her life. She had been attacked in her own condo late Saturday night. The journalist reported that an intruder had crawled through an unlocked window and had slit her throat from "ear to ear."

The ER doctor told the paper if her wounds had been half an inch deeper, she'd have bled out. She had also been raped, beaten with a clothes iron to the face, and stabbed in the left side of her chest, all while in her own bed. The intruder had then drunk a soft drink and watched her television while she lay bleeding. Afterward, he left and tossed the soda can in the grass, and crawled back into his apartment window. In custody was twenty-year-old Lawrence Wayne Buford.

I immediately felt nauseated and could hardly breathe. I suddenly realized I had been in the presence of a real murderer. There was no pretending he was some nice guy who did something bad just once. My legs shook uncontrollably and I knew I could not stand up.

A year later, they held the trial for this assault. They never had mine. The district attorney was satisfied with the two life sentences Buford received for the one crime. I was offered a photojournalist job with a newspaper in central Texas and moved away. I met and married a wonderful officer in the Air Force, got my daughter back, and had a son a year later.

I never forgot what happened to me that spring night in April 1989. My faith in God has been restored after that night. I stopped looking to men for validation. I learned that my Heavenly Father is whom I can truly trust and love, and who loves me in return.

I am not afraid of dying. I know from that night, from that brief moment feeling peace and safety, that I experienced just a glimpse of what is in store for us in heaven.

The other day I looked up Lawrence Wayne Buford's profile on the Texas

Department of Corrections website. I learned he is in a maximum-security prison located in South Texas, not too far from my home. I sometimes wonder why he threw his life away and if I should write or visit him. I have to say I don't think it is wise. I have a wonderful life, marriage, children, and grandchildren now, twenty-six years later.

In a way I'm sort of glad it happened, because I was at Rock Bottom at the time and now my cup runneth over.

Dixie Dobbins, is an award-winning Certified Master Photographer residing in Houston, Texas. She has photographed the likes of President George. W. Bush, professional athletes, politicians, and numerous families and children. Her work has been published in several professional photography magazines, including **The Professional Photographers of America.** *She is also an author on professional photography techniques and speaks around the country teaching pros the craft of photography. She is married with two grown children and three grandchildren. She enjoys traveling, gardening and boating on the lake. You can learn more about Dixie at http://wwwDixie.blogspot.com*

May you be blessed as you create the life you want & live intentionally!

Misty Gilbert

LIVING INTENTIONALLY IN FREEDOM

Misty Gilbert

May God, the source of hope, fill you with joy and peace through your faith in him. Then you will overflow with hope by the power of the Holy Spirit.

– Romans 15:13 (GW)

In 1997, I would be faced with the choice of whether I wanted to stay in bondage to feelings, emotions, fears, and beliefs by continuing to live under the voice of my parents, or whether I wanted to move forward creating the life that I believed God had for me.

My childhood was anything but nurturing and loving. It was full of control, manipulation, anger, lies, resentment, sarcasm, hard feelings, lack of approval, abuse, stress, criticism, condemnation, disrespect, pride, hypocrisy, and justification on every level.

My pain was physical...

...emotional...

...mental...

...and spiritual...

The only way I ever saw out of this situation was to get married. Having been told no man would ever want me because of the burden of my physical health issues, I didn't have much hope.

However, my life was not nearly as miserable as it was going to get.

At age seventeen, life created a turn of events that dramatically changed my world. Whether you view that I was messing around with a married man twenty-eight years older than me, or that I was taken advantage of sexually and raped, the fact remains that because of this, my parents made my life a living hell. Upon learning of my inappropriate conduct, my dad spit at me from across my parent's bedroom and said he could understand me treating him this way, but not my mom.

Because of my actions, I was now considered a slave within my family with limited options. I no longer shared a bedroom with my sister. I was moved to a sleeping bag at the foot of my parents' bed until a partition was made in the dining room for a twin bed with about one and a half feet on each side of it for a walkway. I had one pillow, sheets, and a thin blanket. None of my normal bedding was allowed. I was allowed a lamp, a bookcase, and a picture frame of a friend I admired. I was only allowed my Bible. There were no other reading materials until my mom provided me two books I had to read to deal with my issues of sexual misconduct.

My wardrobe was reduced to five outfits (which made getting through a week difficult to nearly impossible as we had strict days we did certain loads of laundry). All my high heels, nylons, hair bows, necklaces, bracelets, watches, and nice clothing were taken away—the goal was a simple look. Any hobbies, books, crafts, stationary for letter writing, playing the piano, or other fun things were no longer options I was allowed to do.

My bath towel could not hang next to my siblings like it always had because I was completely contaminated. I was not allowed to have any juice, sweets, purified water, or any food considered of higher quality. My parents made me give them all my money as I wasn't trusted to have anything in my possession. I no longer received my weekly allowance. My parents changed their credit card numbers and checking account numbers, as they believed I was a criminal and couldn't be trusted.

I no longer could have my birth control pills (which were my life-saving grace for unbelievable monthly periods that were heavy, painful, and involved vomiting each month for days). Though I bled profusely for three weeks and was told the man I'd been involved with had had a vasectomy, my mom was sure I was pregnant. She made sure that I knew that if I became a mother, they would not financially support my child or me. She also informed me that she would not have a Hispanic grandchild and would not claim it as her grandchild if I had the baby.

Life was miserable on a whole new level. I was not allowed to converse over meals with the family; I had to eat in silence. Extra leaves were put in the table so I sat at the end all by myself in order to feel more secluded. I was not allowed to have any leisure time. I worked from the minute my mom woke me up, around 6 a.m., until it was time to go to bed, around 9 p.m. As I was now considered the family slave, I did all laundry, all cooking, and all cleaning. When the chores were done, I was given the task of cleaning each and every book on the numerous bookshelves my dad had—inside both covers, the binding, the edges, etc. The house was cleaned in ways it never had been.

My eighteenth birthday was four months later, but I was not allowed to celebrate it because I didn't deserve any attention, love, celebration, or gifts. The day before my eighteenth birthday, my parents removed all medications I was on for my heart condition and allergies (cold turkey), because they did not believe that I had had enough of a change of heart in four months. I was threatened daily with eviction; they warned me they would put my bags and me in the street. This threat was horrific as I knew nobody and had no friends where we lived.

My parents were also deeply concerned that I had AIDS, and so I went through AIDS testing at the public health department every six months for three-and-a-half years, even with negative results. The health department told my mom this wasn't necessary if there were no additional encounters, but she didn't believe they knew what they were talking about as she had read documentation to the contrary. My mom was angry that she had to go to such a lowly place with me, that I would do such a horrible thing to her by making her take me there, how her reputation was being affected by my conduct, and that I would risk

exposing her to such a disease. I was constantly reminded that if I had AIDS, they were going kick me out of the house.

I was full of intense fear regarding my future and my health. I was told that I deserved to be beaten and killed like Jesus was, and my mom would proceed to slap me nonstop the entire drive to the clinic to give me a taste of what it was like to receive punishment that you deserved. I had to wear latex gloves in the kitchen while cooking so that I would not contaminate their food. I developed a severe rash on both arms due to an allergy to the latex, and my arms became infected. My mom refused to buy any creams or lotions to provide relief, as this was additional punishment. As a slave, I had given up all my rights to being treated like a civilian with healthcare options.

My parents made it clear that if I ever got married, my wedding dress would be black unless I had a complete change of heart. However, they constantly chastised me that there was no way it ever would be white because I was not pure and could not pretend I was.

My driver's license was revoked. I was no longer called by my legal name of Misty. I was called Ethel (my mom thought that was a horrible name and stated I had lost all right to be called by the God-given name I'd had). She reinforced this by taking my Olan Mills baby pictures and tearing them in half and informing me that I was no longer her beautiful first-born child. I was used and would never be wanted, trusted, respected, or loved by anyone and that she disowned me. I was now considered the last born of the family and if anything ever needed to be done with her and dad or their estate, it would be done by my sister and brother who were now considered the first- and second-born children.

When we went to church, I was treated like a child and had to stay by my mom's side at all times. I was allowed to have no personal conversations with anyone because I had given up the right to have any friendships since I was such a horrible person and a bad influence. After nine months of "proving myself," my parents required me to give a public confession at church. Some of my punishment lessened at this point, and I was allowed to eat with the family. Though I still was not allowed to be alone with my brother or sister, I got a little bit of free time, along with the fact that we had a small celebration for my eighteenth birthday.

This was my life for the next three-and-a-half years, until I came to Texas for a Christian camp retreat and the opportunity to visit my sister who had moved to Texas six weeks previously. This was my first time away from my parents by my own choice, my first time to fly (I was only allowed to fly by accompanying an older couple my parents approved of), and my first time to Texas.

Before my trip, my parents made me promise not to talk to any of the church leadership about the problems at home, as they did not believe it was any of their business. During the extended weekend Christian camp retreat, one of the Fort Worth, Texas ministers asked to spend some time with me to confirm some things my sister had told him since moving to Texas. I was very reserved, but agreed with the understanding that I was not going to offer any other information.

This man went over many scriptures in God's Word to help me see things differently, not under the gaze of my parents who believed that I had to live at home my entire life and fulfill my seven-year sentence, unless I got married. This was the beginning of many life-changing things as it provided me a new way of viewing the things I had experienced in my childhood, my purpose in life, and my beliefs. It made me question whose voice I was listening to and if I would trust God.

I was to be in Texas for a week, but after being out of the cruel, abusive environment I had known all my life, I experienced a bit of peace and freedom that I had never known before and it was affecting me. The night before I was to leave, I was overcome with anxiety and fear because I knew one thing for certain—I did not want to go home to what I knew as "home." I didn't know what my options were and felt confusion at even remotely trying to figure out what was the right thing to do, but I knew with all my heart what I didn't want.

In discussing things with the older couple I flew out with and church leadership, it was decided the best thing for me to do was extend my trip to help me figure things out. We called my parents and informed them that I was having a really great time and needed more time in Texas.

These people stayed on the phone when my parents requested to speak with me and got to hear first hand their response. I was told that if I lost my job, they would not financially support me, and that if I lost my health insurance, they would not pay my medical bills.

After making that initial decision, things moved rather quickly as I took action. I created a resume, went on job interviews, located a place to live in Texas, and made plans to go home and get my things. I knew that this was a huge decision, a risky choice that might not yield the results I so desperately wanted, but I also knew that nothing could be worse than what I had experienced thus far.

I had nothing to lose.

The catch was to plan things so that I didn't put myself in a situation that caused me more physical or emotional pain than I already faced by cutting ties with my parents and everything that had been a security to this point in my life.

We drove all night to California. I notified my parents the night before I was to get my things that I was in town and would be by the next day to have a discussion. We rode up to my parent's house in a thirteen-passenger van with all the seats taken out so we could load up all my things. The men sat up front in the bucket seats and us ladies sat in lawn chairs. (Even in 1997, I'm not sure how we did this in California with the seat-belt laws!)

On the way to my parents, I got my crafts out of the store I had them on consignment in, got my final paycheck from my employer, closed out my bank account, and went to have a meeting with two couples from church. Upon arriving at my parents' home, we had a three-hour discussion in which my parents told me that if I made this decision to leave, I was never welcome back in their home; I would be leaving without their blessing. My mom informed me that the church people would never help me, and that I would be dead within two years due to my health issues if I moved from the desert. I made it very clear that I was fine with this as there had not been any love, happiness, peace, forgiveness, or harmony at home, and that I was going to try something new. My parents had never treated me with respect, would not forgive me if I did not finish out my seven-year sentence, and would literally disown me if I followed through with this decision, yet I believed with all my heart that it was necessary and that God was calling me to move on and be set free.

Since embarking on my new life in September 1997, I have had lessons to learn, heartaches to work through, lies to face, beliefs to change, struggles to overcome, and truth to understand. By making this one step in my leap of faith to trust that God had provided a new path for me, even if that meant leaving everything and everyone I had ever known, I was taking control of my own life to be intentional in my pursuit to create the life that I wanted, one that was empowered by His love, grace and forgiveness.

You have to be willing to stop and ask these questions: What is truth? Whose voice am I listening to? Will you completely trust an all-knowing God? Then you will be able to approach all areas of life with new eyes as to what it means to please the Lord and not others. When you are willing to honestly move from trying to live a life to meet the expectations of everyone else, in fear of making a mistake, choosing to fight the voices that you are not good enough even when you aim for perfection, and believing you matter and are loved, then you can live in the moment, intentionally, with courage, freedom, and truth. This requires you to remove the mask, face the pain, find your voice, and be willing to create new patterns and beliefs.

I know that Rock Bottom is a beautiful place because it is through my horrific experiences that I have been able to understand that all our experiences shape us to be who we are. I have learned that through my painful experiences of rejection and abandonment, I have an ability to show love and comfort to others because I relate to their pain. We are all working through these experiences to find the truth, accept love, have courage, and share grace. It is through facing the dark days when I thought I couldn't make it another moment that I have found that God gives me the power to choose whose voice I listen to and to not give in to those negative thoughts. God gives me the courage, wisdom, strength, and focus to face these things that I couldn't control and to learn to have gratitude even in the midst of pain. Through these moments, I refuse to be a product of my past because I believe in a God who can heal all things broken! I will be courageous, generous, and loving!

Through the years, my relationship with God has deepened, and I have come to know and understand His unconditional love in a different way than I knew Him as a child. I believe He wants the very best for me in spite of any difficulties, pain, and sorrow experienced through an unloving and abusive childhood. Learning that people can't love you beyond the love they have for themselves helped me to learn to love and accept myself. This simple shift can change the way you respond to others, your demeanor, and outlook towards life.

Without forgiveness, it is impossible to move on in life. Learning to come to peace with the things someone has done to you doesn't mean you still don't have feelings or emotions that can be brought up to the surface very quickly with the remembrance of circumstances, things said, or actions. As simplistic as this is, sometimes you have to realize that your only option is to just walk away. They have the power to choose just as much as you do, and their decisions are not a reflection on you. The power lies in how you choose to let these situations affect you.

It is my prayer that you, too, may come to a place of peace with regard to your life and your part in anyone else's life. Put the past behind you so that you may press on to live a life full of abundance in His blessings and obtain freedom, because His power is phenomenal! Learn to live in and with God.

Misty Gilbert has been an entrepreneur as a Medical Practice Consultant providing consulting, training, accounting, and medical billing services for eleven years to her clients. Her focus is to assist small businesses and medical practices with improving their platform, developing team skills, assisting with industry changes, and helping them improve and define their processes to increase profit. Misty lives in Texas and enjoys spending time entertaining friends, building relationships, and pursuing those things she is passionate about, particularly travel, reading, knitting, and pool time! To connect with Misty, visit www.medicalaccountsolutions.com, www.facebook.com/mistywgilbert, www.instagram.com/mistywgilbert and www.twitter.com/mistywgilbert

SECOND CHANCES

Cindy Hatella

*"For I know the plans I have for you," declares the Lord,
"plans to prosper you and not to harm you, plans to give
you hope and a future."*

– Jeremiah 29:11 (NIV)

Like many young women, I was looking for the fairy tale, to find my prince charming and live happily ever after. What I didn't know then is that I was looking for something to fill the God-sized hole in my heart. I really wasn't even aware it was there. But I was turning to everything that wouldn't fill that hole in my heart—dating, drinking, and things that didn't satisfy.

As a child I went to church every Sunday, but always wondered about the big Bible sitting in the back of the end table in the corner. Sometimes I was curious and pulled it out to look at it. Little did I know that in the covers of that book contained everything I needed to live my life.

I was somewhat shy, insecure, and self-conscious as a young girl, and it carried into high school and beyond. I often compared myself to others. I think this may have been due to being teased. I often felt like there was something wrong with me. I wish I'd been told then that God loved me just the way I was, and I was perfect in His eyes.

I wasn't sure what I wanted to do with my life after I graduated from high school so that fall, I went to Colorado with a couple of friends and spent the winter working at a ski resort. (I would not recommend this to my children, based on my experience there.) There was a great deal of alcohol and drug activity. I am grateful that I was protected from developing a desire to get involved with drugs.

After I returned home to Wisconsin, I wasn't sure what I wanted to do with my life and still didn't have direction. I had always been a dreamer, and many of the things I expressed wanting to do when I graduated I was told were big dreams that I should probably forget—they weren't possible. The things I heard seemed to guide my life and hold me back. But I chose to listen to the negative voices.

I worked at a couple of different jobs, a few years passed, and I eventually made the decision to go to tech school so I could get a good job. I was in a relationship right around that time with a man who was brought up in a Christian family, and I chose to end that relationship.

I started tech school and later met a man whom I eventually married. I had the strange notion that a man would make me happy. I wish I had learned sooner that you had to be whole before going into a marriage. Two going into a marriage carrying baggage did not make for a good combination. It was a great marriage until about eight to nine years into it when it started going downhill. At this time, God was knocking on my heart's door, and I wanted nothing but to devote my life and my marriage to Him, so I did. Two great Christian friends helped me during this time. They encouraged me to read my Bible and to read Christian books that would help me grow in my newfound faith.

It was hard at home, and some nights I would stop at the grocery store or the Christian bookstore before I went home. I was searching for answers. My husband accused me of things that weren't happening. Through a series of events and much deception, it was revealed to me that my husband was seeing someone else. I wanted to work it out, but there was no sign of that happening. Before our tenth anniversary, we were divorced.

During the many years following my divorce, my children and I went through some very difficult times. My son was living with his father and my daughter was living with me. The reasons for this were not in the best interest of the children, and it put a huge strain on all of us! With all the emotions I was experiencing, I needed to become emotionally healthy. This is where I truly began to see God was working in my life (or was it that I hadn't noticed it before this time?). I realized later that, had I been focusing on the Lord and His plan for my life and putting my trust in Jesus, much of the emotional strain could have been avoided.

I experienced a myriad of emotions as I walked through that painful experience. I was feeling fear, anger, rejection, shame, and loss. It took many years to work though all of them. If I'm honest with myself, there are layers that God is still peeling away...but I think that we all continue to be "peeled" throughout our walk in this short journey we call "life." This experience really made me forget who I was. I am grateful to Him for His love and not letting me remain in that place of fear, hurt, and rejection. He wants us to be like Him and there is nothing I want more.

It seemed as I was on the journey through these years, God continually put new Christians in my path, in my life, and in places of assistance where He knew I needed them. I would comment almost weekly about this person or that person that we'd just met and who had impacted us somehow. The people in the church we were going to at the time turned out to be our guardian angels, and I am so thankful for everything they did to help us. This made an incredible impact on my life and the lives of my children. I will be forever grateful. So many of my friends were thoughtful, caring, and supportive. Even the times I was angry and not making good decisions, they stayed by my side and didn't judge. They just loved me like Jesus does and they never gave up on me.

I would be remiss if I didn't mention that many of my actions in my anger and fear were not of benefit to my kids. I hurt their feelings during my bouts of anger, and I wish I could wipe those times away. I couldn't see outside myself because I was hurting and because of the pain. I became self-focused and didn't really know what to do with it. I did a lot of yelling for a period of time. They remember, but they have forgiven me. For that I will be eternally grateful to God. I am thankful for God's forgiveness.

I am very grateful for the restoration that He has done in my life. This verse that was given to me by one of my sisters in Christ still has so much meaning to me. She encouraged me to live on this promise.

> I will repay you for the years the locusts have eaten—the great locust and the young locust, the other locusts and the locust swarm—my great army that I sent among you. Joel 2:25 (NIV)

God is a God of restoration and if I focus on Him, He is faithful and just to fulfill His promises. God brought me to a beautiful place where I didn't need a person to fulfill me. Of course, that's the time when He brought my husband to me. In the first five minutes after we met, we were talking about the Bible. That was a good sign!

However, I still wasn't really ready for a relationship. And my husband gave me space before he even asked me out. He waited about six months before our first date, which fell on his birthday.

I believe God brought us together for a purpose and I believe if we seek Him with all our heart, soul, mind, and strength, our marriage will be a beautiful testimony of His faithfulness. I am amazed at how He strengthens us and helps us change those parts of us that aren't honoring to Him. He desires for us to have a deep relationship with Him and that is what I seek. I want to honor Him with the life He has given me.

Take delight in the LORD, and he will give you the desires of your heart. Psalm 37:4 (NIV)

The fairy tale has come true in my life! We have been married almost ten years and he is a blessing beyond what I could have imagined. God knows just what we need. We share similar dreams and are in a new season in our lives, and with that comes pursuing those dreams together. We encourage each other to pursue our own personal dreams also. It is an exciting journey and I am so grateful for everything God has done in my life. My kids are amazing, and I continue to be in awe as I watch them grow and chase the dreams God has put in their hearts. I am truly blessed!

The song "Bless the Broken Road" really resonates with my heart. My husband and I each had baggage coming into our marriage, but we have been so blessed now that we know the Lord as our Savior!

I know that Rock Bottom is a beautiful place because I have learned how to be truly grateful to God, even in the hard times.

Cindy Hatella has been employed at a utility for twenty-eight years. She is building a Shaklee business and runs a mobile wood-fired pizza business with her husband, and they are quickly becoming known as the "pizza man and pizza lady." She is passionate about encouraging others to realize the beauty God has placed within them, to know they are loved and adored by God, and to see the beauty of the dreams God has placed in their hearts. She wants to inspire women to be courageous and follow their God-given dreams. She lives on the lake with her wonderful husband and happy-go-lucky golden retriever, Bob. She is blessed with two amazing and talented children—a son and daughter!

ROCK BOTTOM IS A BEAUTIFUL PLACE 3

BLESSINGS OF A BROKEN HEART

Heather Hobbs

It was so that the works of God might be displayed in him.
– John 9:3b (NASB)

My story of a grateful heart begins with a broken one. I was born to a young couple who already had a little boy. My older brother was very energetic and intelligent. He was a true handful. My parents were proud to have him and were eagerly awaiting the birth of their second child. My mother did not have a sonogram to know whether I was a boy or a girl, so as all parents respond when asked what gender they prefer, my parents would say, "We don't care as long as the baby is healthy."

Well, my parents learned what happens when the baby isn't healthy. I was born on October ninth, and my parents were excited to see that I was a precious little girl. The first day they spent with me was full of bliss and pure excitement, but the second day proved to be drastically different. As my mom recovered in the hospital, my pediatrician came in to talk to her. He told her that the nurse had heard a murmur when listening to my heart. At the time, no one knew how life changing that moment would be for my entire family. Three weeks later, my mom rushed my limp body to the hospital where she learned that I was in congestive heart failure.

Years later, I was diagnosed with a rare syndrome called Shone's syndrome. Most of those diagnosed with this set of defects do not live to adulthood. I had the defects of this syndrome along with others and arrhythmias. My parents experienced a wide range of emotions as they learned more and more about the debilitating heart defects I had. Each day became a blessing (as I was still alive), and my parents went on to have two more healthy boys.

My life growing up was very different than most people's experience. I wasn't able to play with my friends and brothers the same way everyone else did, but I still had fun and didn't mind the difference. I knew my life was limited and believed that I could die at any minute, but I loved my life and was grateful for it. When I was eight years old, my aortic valve became narrowed to the point that it was causing me to be very ill. After going to a doctor's appointment in Houston, it was determined that I needed to have a procedure called a *valvuloplasty*. The doctors would run a catheter up my veins from my groin area, to my heart, and then blow a balloon up into the valve to tear away the extra tissue that was causing the narrowing of the aorta. This procedure was new, and I was going to be the doctor's eighth patient. Even at my young age, I understood that this procedure was dangerous and there was a chance I would not live. My parents were always good about keeping me in every doctor's appointment so I heard what the doctors were telling them. I am glad they kept me informed, but it also meant I knew the reality of every procedure and event in my life.

As I was preparing to have the procedure done, I went to my grandparents' house on Lake Bridgeport. My family took a boat ride to enjoy the lake. My Grandma loved to quote scripture and pray and was very demonstrative about her faith. I was on the boat with her and she began to quote the twenty-third psalm. She began with the first verse: "The Lord is my shepherd, I shall not want." (NASB)

I stopped my Grandma and said, "So, I shouldn't want my heart to get better?" I thought of "shall not" in the context of *you shall not murder* or *you shall not steal.*

Grandma explained to me that the verse meant God provides everything we need. There is nothing more we need than what He has already given us. I didn't need to be a healthy little girl. I didn't need to have a heart that worked. I didn't need anything but what God had already supplied for me. I didn't need anything but God.

I realized that with God I was complete and whole. Gratitude filled me as I was able to understand the true love of God and what it means to be whole. In that moment I was grateful for the sufficiency of God.

As my life continued, I had years that were good and I wasn't as sick, and I had years that were not good and I was truly suffering. I had open-heart surgery at the age of thirteen when my aortic valve began to fail. I was new to the school I was attending in the seventh grade. It was a private Christian school with a class of about seventy-five, but I still didn't know everyone that well and felt out of place. Then as the second half of the school year started, I became ill. The doctors originally felt they would need to give me a heart transplant. In 1991, that was still a very new procedure and it was not well established. I was in total shock with no idea how to process it. I came back to school and told my classmates and teachers. The doctors decided to try open-heart surgery and replace my aortic valve, and rebuild my aorta with a Dacron® patch.

That time in my life was very terrifying, and I wasn't sure how to deal with it. I overheard my mom telling my teachers and heard their reaction as they were in tears. I also got to see how my classmates reacted and rallied around me. Through that experience I was able to understand the love of God shining through others. I was so overcome by the love of others that I was overwhelmed. In those moments, I was grateful for the Christian community.

As I grew up, I was able to experience many new things, including going to Europe, mission trips, college, and grad school. I was sick through many of those years, but I was not willing to let my health stop me from doing the things God has called me to do. I was very ill all through college and graduate school, but I knew God had a purpose for me.

After I received my master's degree from Dallas Theological Seminary, my health was better than it had ever been and I was doing wonderfully. I was thrilled to be able to be involved with friendships and work. In 2008 that began to change as my health failed. I had to stop working and move in with my parents, giving up my independence. I went through three procedures and a stroke and nothing worked; my heart was still failing. My two grandfathers passed away, and the man I had been dating for almost two years broke up with me. I was losing hope. That was the only time in my life that I can point to and say I was truly depressed.

I had no idea how to handle it, but I had a friend who had gone through a hard time recently, and I was talking to him about all of my issues. He said to me, "Heather, you believe God is good, right?" I said "Yes!" Then Josh said, "If God is good, then His plans are good. If His plans are good, then His plans for you are good. Heather, you either believe it or you don't." In that moment I realized my depression and sorrow were really the sin of unbelief. It was my way of not trusting God that He is who He says that He is. Sadness in itself is not a sin, but being sad to the point where you don't trust God is a sin. In that moment, I was grateful for the honesty of a friend.

I continued to become sicker over time and had to continue to live at home with my parents. I no longer had a social life or a work life. I was just trying to survive. It became obvious that the only thing that would keep me alive was to have a heart transplant. After several procedures and hoops, I was finally placed on the heart transplant waiting list in 2012. I waited for a year until I became so sick that I had to be hospitalized in ICU with IV drugs going into my neck. I was in the hospital for five weeks until one day, the doctors came in and told me that there was a possible heart available, and it was between me and one other person. I tried so hard to not get my hopes up. I waited for several hours to know if it would be my heart.

All of my life I would wish and hope for the ability to feel a normal heartbeat. I would pray and ask God to just let me feel a normal heartbeat one time in my life, if even just for a few moments. I thought with this new heart I could finally get my wish. This heart would be my only chance to stay alive, to watch my family grow, to spend time with friends, my chance to make my life count.

The resident doctor came into the room a few hours later and told me the heart had gone to someone else. The devastation I felt in that moment is beyond words. In the first few minutes, I couldn't even process it. I sat there in silence as a thought came to me that could only be from the Lord. I thought, *I can either choose to be angry, bitter, sad—and no one would blame me—or I can choose to believe this is God's will for my life and count it as joy.* In that moment, I made the choice to count it as joy and stated out loud that this was God's will for my life. In that moment, I was grateful for the Holy Spirit.

Three days later, a heart became available that would go to me. When they told me that the heart would be mine, uncontrolled tears started falling and wouldn't stop. They were tears of pure exhilaration. I had no fear, no trepidation, because I had nothing to lose. I received the heart of a young man. I was and I am grateful for my donor and his family.

After my transplant, I began to wonder what I was going to do with the rest of my life. I knew God had saved me multiple times for something greater than I could understand. I desperately wanted to be living in the will of God. God led me to John 9:1-3 "As He passed by, He saw a man blind from birth. And His disciples asked Him, 'Rabbi, who sinned, this man or his parents, that he would be born blind?' Jesus answered, 'It was neither that this man sinned, nor his parents; but it was so that the works of God might be displayed in him.'" (NASB)

As a child, I always loved this story because the man was healed. As I got older, it gave me comfort that I hadn't done anything wrong and my parents hadn't done anything wrong to cause my heart problems. The last part of these verses did not hit me until after transplant. I realized that God gave me my heart problems to show others His good works in my life. I realized that those works wouldn't be shone unless I told others of them. With that, I started a non-profit called Twice Loved Heart. I tell my story to churches, women's groups, Bible studies, and anyone else who is willing to listen.

I had complications post-transplant and had to go to the Mayo clinic to get a second opinion. At that time, I met a man who also had congenital heart defects and was told he would need a heart/liver transplant. I was able to help him through the emotional processes of that week. I realized that God had a second plan for my non-profit. I began life coaching and mentoring congenital heart defect patients and organ transplant patients. I believe this gives me the chance to show others the love of God in a way that most could never understand. I am grateful for the chance to love others.

Through my experiences, I have learned to be grateful for so much in life. I am grateful for my family and especially my parents who have stood by me every step of the way. I am grateful for my friends, church, and the Christian community who have showed me the love of God. I am grateful to the Lord for carrying me through the darkest moments in my life. I am grateful to be alive and enjoy my family. I am grateful for my donor and his family. With all of that, I am most grateful that God chose me to have the honor of being the one to walk this difficult path. Without the lessons I have learned through my experience of suffering, I would not be the woman I am today, but more importantly, I would not have the ability to serve others in my uniquely gifted way. I am forever grateful!

Heather Hobbs is the Founder and Ministry Director of a non-profit called Twice Loved Heart. Her desire is to encourage others that even in the most difficult of times, they can live with the joy of the Lord. She has a bachelor's in social work from Texas Christian University and a master's in biblical counseling from Dallas Theological Seminary. www.twicelovedheart.com

RELEASE ME

Melissa Hohnstreiter

Something is NOT better than nothing, because that "something" can leave you with nothing.

– Melissa Hohnstreiter

I sat at home, plagued with feelings of shame, anxiety, loneliness, and immense fear. If I could have just slept it all away, I would have. However, the sleep was only a short escape from the emotions and uncertainty of my future. The pain and agony of not being enough for someone to love, yet again, rocked my life, my confidence, and my sanity.

I loved this man and I was certain he was the one God had brought into my life to love me and protect me. I was not a woman with much identity or confidence, so when I experienced this man's love for me, I held on to it tightly, and I made sure I wouldn't do anything to disappoint or cause him not to want me. I knew he had to be God's will for me, even though I was coming out of a divorce when I started dating him. I gave myself no time to heal, to learn from the mistakes made, or allow God to do His work in me. On the rebound, without godly counsel or talking with others, I secretly married what would be my fourth husband.

Again, certain this marriage was "the one," I did everything I could to be a godly wife, supportive, and loving in every way possible. I tried to be perfect—it is in my DNA. I continued to participate in the same activities as I did before we married. However, I began to notice when I left for the gym to teach aerobics, he would become irritated and try to make me feel guilty. I was educated and a teacher at the time, which I felt made him feel insecure about himself. As time went on, he would play mind games with me. He would move my things and act like he had no idea what I was talking about. I would believe him, thinking he wouldn't do these things to me, and chalked it up to maybe me being careless. He was a police officer in our town, a well thought of policeman. I supported him and encouraged him to pursue a higher education. The more I tried to love him, support him, and be the wife he would want, the more he became cynical, sadistic, and manipulative.

My greatest fear was failing at this marriage, and living with the embarrassment. Because of this, the more manipulative and sadistic he became, the greater my fears grew. He sensed my fear of being alone and failing again and capitalized on them. I ratchetted up my attempts to make everything perfect. The mind games only got worse, and he became very physical. I kept everything a secret from my friends and family. My only thought was to keep everything perfect, be supportive, and not rock the boat. As long as I didn't rock the boat, then he would stay, right?

I believe I took responsibility for everything, good or bad. I remember waking up in the middle of the night and processing all of the days' events, and I would get angry at myself for allowing the chaos to continue and allowing him to mentally and physically abuse me. I would ask myself why, why? I just didn't want to let go. I recall saying, "I just can't fail again." At times, I would find myself so angry and wanting to quit, and then other times, I was so scared of being by myself. In my mind, "something was better than nothing," so I continued on living a lie and living in fear of abandonment, all the while losing my mind. Did I mention, I am a Christian and do believe in God? I even tithed my paycheck while I was married to this man.

I continued to live in the chaos, lies, and deception. The mental abuse became far worse than I thought it ever could, but I always lived with the hopes he would stop. We went to counseling one time. I had one question to ask him in front of the counselor. "Why won't you say I am pretty?" His reply was: "I don't know," and he laughed. No emotion, no care that I wanted and needed to hear that I was pretty. No vulnerability, no nothing. The counselor later told me I should prepare to move on from him. Still in disbelief, I continued anything and everything I could to make it work. I continued to endure the humiliation, mental and physical abuse, and emotional abuse.

That is, until one day, when my life literally flashed before my eyes.

He was extremely frustrated with me because I needed his help preparing our health insurance plans. As he continued to watch television, unaffected by the information needed, he looked at me with such disdain in his eyes. He began yelling at me, and I kept quiet for a minute. Then, I lost it completely.

That's when he came at me. He picked me up by my neck, and I literally came off the floor. He began choking me. It wasn't until he tripped and lost his grip on me that I got away. He told me he could kill me and get away with it. That was it—enough was enough. He left because I was going to call 911 on him, a police officer. He cared about his job more than he did me.

Living with him was only part of my hell. In spite of the near-death experience I had just faced, I was plagued with my continuous thoughts and fears, and wanted to keep all the abuse a secret so no one would see I had failed at a marriage once again. I was so ashamed, lost, and embarrassed, and I had no idea who to turn to without judgment. To the best of my ability, I kept it all to myself. Thank God for work. That kept my mind a little busy, but not much. I was losing weight because I felt sick to my stomach all the time. I couldn't wait to get home, close the garage door, and go into hiding...then to sleep. Sleep was only a small break from my thoughts.

One night the pain of the secrets became way too much to bear. I couldn't cry enough, couldn't stop the racing thoughts, couldn't stop the sickness in my stomach, and couldn't manage the various emotions. I found myself twisting and twisting my hair, and just couldn't stop. In this black hole of pain, I took a broken piece of tile and cut the outside of my thigh. It felt so good. Yes, as crazy as it sounds, it felt SO good. For the first time in many, many years, I felt a release of everything I had caged up, so I did it several times that night. I didn't want to live through the pain again, but I didn't want to die. I just need to feel better.

This became my secret coping mechanism for several months. However, it didn't do much for the racing thoughts, and I finally reached out to a friend, sharing what was going on and where I was mentally and emotionally. I just wanted the pain to end and there was no end. As always, I was looking for a sure fix. I even hoped he would come back because the pain was something I avoided most my life. Just like before, I would just move and not allow myself to deal or heal.

Consequently, this time was different. I was emotionally bankrupt, with no will or energy to move forward on my own. I knew I needed help. As messed up as cutting was, it helped me feel for a short time, but I knew I had to learn to express my thoughts, feelings, and emotions in the appropriate way. Most importantly, my thoughts had to change; my belief system had to change. I was going to have to let God change me this time. My decision-making skills had left me void of any self-esteem, void of acceptance for myself, and most of all, lacking any identity.

I learned as a young girl I had to be perfect before my parents would show me any form of love. As a young girl, I got into trouble a lot and so, wasn't shown much love. I look back on my life, and it is safe to say I had no direction, was a little lost, and only knew performance-based love. Therefore, most of my adulthood, I became whatever I needed to be to gain love and acceptance. Obviously, it didn't matter whose love, as long as I got some. After this last marriage, I asked myself why I had hung on for so long. I had always felt that love was in short supply for me, so I guess I felt like I needed to stay with my husband because I didn't know when the next time love would come around. That was such messed up thinking. My philosophy was "something was better than nothing." The irony behind that ridiculous statement is that "something" took everything and left me with nothing.

I am a Christian who feared man more than I did God. Man was my idol, not God. This understanding was a smack in the face to me. However, the thought of not being someone's wife, significant other, or being alone brought my fear to the point I mutilated my legs terribly and later attempted suicide. I couldn't see past the immediate, and the uncertainty literally drove me crazy. This time of being alone seemed to last an eternity, and I wanted to hurry up and fix myself so I could look for my next relationship. Luckily, my husband wasn't coming back, and I knew in my heart that I needed to walk through this.

Many months were spent alone with just me, my thoughts, and God. At first it was very difficult because I sought Him out over and over, wanting answers for how I could fix myself. Oh, how I must have made Him laugh over and over. I kept pursuing God for answers, but as I grew tired of doing so, I stopped striving and asking. I started living my life with hopes of learning and hearing from God. Still, many times, I would overthink things instead of allowing God to show me and teach me.

Before I knew it, I had become content with myself and the stillness. I knew I had put man before God. I learned I had compromised everything I believed and knew in my heart just so I would not be alone. This was my rock bottom experience. However, God was so amazing to me during this time of my life. Only after I surrendered did I get to experience God's truth about myself, experience His love and compassion for me, and allow Him to bring me from darkness into the light.

I know my rock bottom experience is a beautiful place because God used this experience to stop me from going around the mountain— again and again. He showed me truth and helped me strengthen my identity in the process. The fear of being alone is still very real at times. However, hitting rock bottom is a constant reminder of who I really am, and I should never compromise, out of fear, who God has created me to be. As a result of my surrender and God's hard work, I live with much gratitude for all He has done for me. My mission is to share God's truth and help other women come to know that truth.

Gratitude is what I live with today. Had I not trusted God and His work, I would have not have met my fifth, and last husband, John. God used my rock bottom experience to shape and mold me so I could receive His unconditional love and support. I am grateful to God and those who He put in my path to support me, love me through my craziness, and celebrate my victory. I celebrate the fun and love of seven years of marriage this year. I am head over heels in love!

Melissa Hohnstreiter is a high school counselor with a Masters in Education, married to the MOST amazing and supportive husband, and has three phenomenal boys. Her dream is to use her story and her passion to educate, motivate, and foster God's truth to those individuals wanting freedom.

I WILL WALK WITH YOU

Benita Ibrahim

Who comforts us in all our troubles, so that we can comfort those in any trouble with the comfort we ourselves receive from God.

– 2 Corinthians 1:4 (NIV)

My Rock Bottom experience of walking alone through a season of my life led me to "living with a grateful heart. " I think we all go through different seasons in our life—seasons of joy, seasons of grief, seasons of weeping, seasons of regret, seasons of doubt, seasons of change, seasons of hope, and seasons of just walking through, because you simply don't know what else to do but walk through. As you continue to walk by faith over the hills and valleys of life, coming out on the other side and reaching the promised land, you began to realize and understand it was all worth it, because you have a greater heart of thanksgiving and the experience hopefully made you a better version of who you are.

As I was reflecting on having a grateful heart and the events that I had to walk through to truly, truly have a grateful heart, it made me think of a very dark season my family and I experienced. It was the most painful season of my life and lasted for several years. It was so painful that we thought God had made a mistake, had the wrong address, and thought that Old Testament patriarch Job lived here!

It was one thing after another, not for just a few months and then sunshine and tap dancing. No, it was one tragedy after another for years with no breather in between. We thought surely this was a bad dream; it couldn't be real. We were actually told by some friends that they thought we were making it up, that no one's life was in constant drama all the time. Because we were the children of God, a royal priesthood, a holy nation, victorious overcomers, filled with the power of the Holy Spirit, maybe there was sin in our lives and God was punishing us for it.

Or, it was suggested, maybe we just liked the attention. That was a good one! Yep! You figured us out—nine pills a day, barely being able to stand or sleep for days on end, a family member cutting and burning themselves constantly, not knowing if you would get that dreaded call that no parent wants to hear...it seemed every time we turned around, it was yet another trial.

Gone from making an abundant income to merely getting by, we almost lost our home and our business. My mother had been diagnosed with terminal breast cancer and we watched this vibrant, vivacious woman slowly revert back to almost child-like behavior. It was so heartbreaking to see someone you adore die a little bit every day, being totally humbled because they were dependent on you to do everything for them.

The pressure of sickness, finances, and family issues took a huge toll on my marriage. My husband and I were separated for almost a year, and we were headed for divorce. It seemed like the more we went through, the more close friends and family (that we really trusted and loved) became tired of listening to us, praying with us, lifting us up, and counseling with us. They began to pull away. They had all become burnt out from hearing about our misfortune and blended family issues.

I remember being in my bedroom one afternoon, crying out to the Lord and asking Him why were we going through such turmoil. I had feelings of such hopelessness, brokenness, and feeling so deserted. I desperately longed for a touch from Him. I felt like the woman with the issue of blood, pressing through the crowd, wondering if I could just step into the very shadow of His footprints, would I be healed? If I could just touch the hem of His garment, would I be made whole? I needed Him to hold me and tell me everything was all right...

I believe we all walk through valleys and have wilderness experiences, times when we don't hear His voice and don't understand His plans for our lives. There were times I so desperately needed comfort from my sisters in Christ, just to know that someone cared and would be willing to walk through this journey with me. I desired someone who would help carry our burdens and partake in our joy. Someone that would just come and sit with me without me having to say a word, but their presence and their heart would speak volumes!

In the Greek, the word "comfort" means to walk alongside. God sent us laborers and midwives (those that believed in us and walked with us through the last trimester of the labor of our pain and prayed us through the birthing process). I believe that we went through that season so we would never forget what it felt like to be in that desert place and alone, and we could become that encouragement and comfort for others going through "their" season of life, walking along beside them until...and not giving up.

It's not always about stuffing God's Word down someone's throat, but having a listening ear or allowing that person to weep, or allowing that sister to climb into bed and sleep while you watch her kids and clean her house so she can be refreshed. Maybe for one sister, it's vacuuming and washing the dishes sacrificially so your sister in Christ can pull away and indulge in self-care, even if for just a one day. It's being Jesus with skin on, doing ordinary things that are a gift to those broken and needing to be restored.

There is a story in Exodus 17:1-16 that is so powerful and made such an impact on the way I view what I'm called to do (be a comforter to those hurting), that it changed my whole perspective on sisterhood. It gave me a greater understanding that out of everyone in my circle, though they may truly love me, there will only be a few select warriors (sisters) that are willing to walk alongside me—side-by-side, hip-to-hip, going into WAR! These are the women that will rise and say, "I will walk with you and I will fight with you until victory is won. I will walk with you no matter how long it takes—I will be there!"

Exodus 17 begins with the Israelites complaining to Moses. They had left Egypt, a land filled with bondage and slavery (which is all they had ever known), and traveled into a land that was unfamiliar to them but gave them the gift of freedom.

Exodus 17:1-16 NIV (emphasis the author's)

The whole Israelite community set out from the Desert of Sin, traveling from place to place as the Lord commanded. They camped at Rephidim, but there was no water for the people to drink. So they quarreled with Moses and said, "Give us water to drink."

Moses replied, "Why do you quarrel with me? Why do you put the Lord to the test?"

But the people were thirsty for water there, and they grumbled against Moses. They said, "Why did you bring us up out of Egypt to make us and our children and livestock die of thirst?"

Then Moses cried out to the Lord, "What am I to do with these people? They are almost ready to stone me."

The Lord answered Moses, "Go out in front of the people. Take with you *some* of the elders of Israel and take in your hand the staff with which you struck the Nile, and go. I will stand there before you by the rock at Horeb. Strike the rock, and water will come out of it for the people to drink." So Moses did this in the sight of the elders of Israel.

And he called the place Massaha and Meribahb because the Israelites quarreled and because they tested the Lord saying, "Is the Lord among us or not?"

The Amalekites came and attacked the Israelites at Rephidim. Moses said to Joshua, "Choose *some* of our men and go out to fight the Amalekites. Tomorrow I will stand on top of the hill with the staff of God in my hands."

So Joshua fought the Amalekites as Moses had ordered, and Moses, Aaron and Hur went to the top of the hill. As long as Moses held up his hands, the Israelites were winning, but whenever he lowered his hands, the Amalekites were winning. When Moses' hands grew tired, they took a stone and put it under him and he sat on it. Aaron and Hur held his hands up— one on one side, one on the other—so that his hands remained steady till sunset. So Joshua overcame the Amalekite army with the sword.

Then the Lord said to Moses, "Write this on a scroll as something to be remembered and make sure that Joshua hears it, because I will completely blot out the name of Amalek from under heaven."

Moses built an altar and called it The Lord is my Banner. He said, "Because hands were lifted up against the throne of the Lord, the Lord will be at war against the Amalekites from generation to generation."

When you read verses five and eight, I would imagine that there were a ton of men that were physically able to fight. In your natural mind you would think, the more men, the better chances at quickly winning the fight.

Well, His ways are not our ways! What was so powerful, what God instructed them to do was to choose only a few, only *some*, only a select few who would be able to stand and win the fight against the Amalekites. In verse eleven, Aaron, Moses, and Hur were instructed that as long as Moses held up his hands, they would win the war. In verse twelve, Moses begins to get tired and lowers his hands and the Amalekites began to advance. So Aaron and Hur grabbed a stone, placed it under Moses so he could rest and relieve some of the pressure! (I would guess that standing on top of a mountain, in the heat, with my hands lifted high over my head, knees wobbling, thirsty, hungry, and needing to go to the bathroom was beyond difficult!) Then they each got on either side of Moses and held up his hands until they *won the war!*

How many times have we been asked to lift someone up in prayer or God has placed someone on our heart to take them a card of encouragement or buy them groceries or simply go to their home and have tea and just listen...? The significance in Aaron and Hur standing on each side of Moses while his strength was being restored is powerful. I believe this is the very definition of comfort—walking alongside of our sister in Christ until her storm is over.

Will you be that *some?* Having to walk through this Rock Bottom experience has not only confirmed my purpose (that I'm called to give comfort and to be a comfort strategist, and fill in the gap whenever I see a need), but it has taught me to live my life with a grateful heart because God is raising up laborers for the harvest that are the chosen *some!*

Benita Ibrahim is an author, speaker, comfort strategist, and philanthropist. She has been a small business owner for over twenty years and is the founder and director of a daycare facility in Texas. Her life's passion is to empower women through her philanthropy work and to bring comfort, encouragement, and healing to women on their life's journey. She strongly believes your pain is your ministry, and your mess is your message. She was a recipient of the 2014 Women Who Inspire Award for HOPE for **Women Magazine**. *She was also featured in the Fall issue of* **HOPE Magazine**'s *"Women in Leadership" issue. Benita resides in Texas with her husband. They have two amazing sons, three beautiful daughters, six grandchildren and two godchildren. You can find out more about Benita at www.beautifulcolorsdaycare.com or connect with her at www.facebook.com/benitaibrahimsolutions or www.BenitaIbrahimSolutions.com*

BROKEN AND CRUSHED TO BEAUTIFUL AND CHERISHED

Diana Journy

The Lord is close to the broken hearted and saves the crushed in Spirit.

– Psalm 34:18 (NIV)

Who can forget the day when they hit rock bottom? Just thinking of the words brings a pain so deep that it paralyzes me. Rock bottom brought my life (and reality as I had known it and believed it to be) to an abrupt end with no hope of the future that I had dreamed, thought of, or desired. That day my life took a 360 degree turn into the depths of despair and hopelessness, throwing me into a pit of darkness with no glimmer of light.

It was July of 2007, but before I go there, let me give you a little history. In 2006, my husband Tim and I celebrated our thirtieth wedding anniversary. Our life was moving upward and dreams were coming true. Tim had a very high level position that paid very well. Our goals of achieving financial success and getting out of the debt that had consumed most of our marriage were finally being realized.

We had just built our dream home in Florida, our youngest was about to graduate from college, and we were planning to travel the world together. Tim's position required overseas travel and I was ready to start traveling with him. We were excited about our future and looking forward to the next thirty years together. We were right on the cusp of the good life and it was exciting. Then...rock bottom!

Tim and I were having a mini getaway. The night before, we had gone to a concert and chosen to get a room instead of driving home that night. It was a beautiful warm July morning in Florida. We sat outside on our balcony, watching the boats on the water while having breakfast. Tim went into the room to get something and came out with a letter. I was so excited to see that he had finally written me.

You see, for the past six months, I felt Tim distancing himself from me. He seemed distracted, uninterested, uncaring, just not in the moment with me. I had tried to talk with him, but when that didn't work, I started to write him letters.

Only he never responded. He would not open up to me or tell me what was going on. He just continued to drift further away from me, leaving me to believe that something was wrong with me. You can imagine how elated I was to see he had a letter. Finally I would hear from him, finally I would get some answers.

But what I heard was not what I expected and especially not what I wanted.

Tim started with, "I'm finally writing you a letter to tell you something I believe you already know. I have been with another woman for the past eight months. We love each other, but I have ended the relationship and decided to work on our marriage and the problems we have..."

He kept reading aloud, not taking his eyes off the paper, but I heard no more. My mind raced with fear and pain. What was he saying? Another woman? He loved her? Problems in our marriage? Everything was jumbled and I couldn't think, I couldn't comprehend. Over and over I heard a voice in my head, saying: "Diana, get up and jump! End this pain, get up, jump!" The thoughts just kept playing over and over, louder and louder—*end it, jump, end it, jump.* Even though I heard it replayed again and again, I could not move. I was paralyzed! My rock bottom was here!

I wish I could say that the rise up from rock bottom was easy or that I did all the right stuff, but I would be lying. The truth is, I was now on the roller coaster ride of a lifetime, and I was not prepared. Where was that manual on how to handle the betrayal of your spouse?

Well, I was about to discover much about myself. And yes, stuff that, if I'm honest, I didn't even want to know. I guess I had been living in a fantasy world and honestly, I was comfortable with that. I had no problem living with disillusionment, choosing to look in the mirror and seeing only what I wanted to see. I guess I thought I could ignore my fears and run from them, but I couldn't.

So, without being asked if I wanted to go on this journey, my journey began. You bet my heels were dug in—this was not part of my plan for my life. Full of pain and fear, I started the long trip up from the depths of darkness and hopelessness into the freedom of light and hope.

I immediately withdrew into myself, hoping to fade away. As was evidenced by my actions that day when I walked out of the room and left Tim behind, I just wandered away. I tried to disappear into the hustle and bustle of the world. Thoughts of the elevator crashing or walking into the direct path of a car on the street or slipping under the ocean water took up residence in my mind. It didn't matter the means, only the ending.

Today, as I write those words, I'm so grateful that I did not act on those thoughts. Yes, in that moment, on that day, it seemed like the only way out was to end it. I was numb and void of any feelings, yet somewhere deep within I so desperately wanted to feel again. To see light instead of the darkness that was all around me. That day and the months ahead, the task of trying to walk through the pit of rock bottom where there was only darkness was impossible. It would be months of my husband and I muddling in the muck of infidelity, the aftereffects of deceit and betrayal. It was not pretty! I have learned that more damage is done after the disclosure than from the infidelity itself. Each of us had pain and we were hurting each other. We did not know how to stop the craziness, and so we continued on the same destructive path.

It would be eight months of up, down, and around and around, until things changed. Then one day, Tim and I were enjoying a beautiful winter respite at the beach, when he told me he was still struggling and not sure he could stay in the marriage. BAM! There came the knife to the heart, excruciating pain. All I could think was, *not again, I can't take any more!* It was rock bottom all over again. I'm sure it goes without saying that the rest of the day was not good.

Later that night, we were sitting on the floor in the office. I begged Tim to give me a fair try, to give me six months, just six months without any contact from the other woman, just him and me with no other distractions. His eyes were empty and tears rolled down his face.

"I'm not sure she will still be there," he said. Those words ignited something in me that night. The next day, while in my quiet time with the Lord, I started to see things differently. It was the start of God opening my eyes to *me*. Yes, this hurt; yes this was unfair; yes, I was a victim of my husband's choices, but I had to look at what I was doing, how I was behaving, and what my reactions were. Did I want to stay in this dark and hopeless pit, or was I going to crawl my way out? I had a choice to make and it was time to accept my reality. I could choose to either stay in the rancid pit of hate and bitterness or rise above it.

There was work for me to do, places of hurt I had to visit, and reality I needed to accept. Early on my journey, I reached out to several friends who had a strong faith. I needed someone to help me try to stay focused and not let the devastation and destruction consume me. Staying focused was not a very easy task for someone who had withdrawn into the depths of pain and despair.

The night after the beach incident, my friend invited me to a prayer group. Five women (who did not know me), laid hands on me, joined in my battle, and lifted me up before God. Wow! God heard the prayers of those prayer warriors that night. As I left that evening, I knew something had changed. I now had some hope and light. No, the circumstances at home had not changed. Tim was still not sure he wanted to stay in our marriage, but my focus had changed. God loved me, God cared that I was carrying this burden, and He cared that someone had hurt me.

Yes, God cared...

I wish I could say it all ended there, but the truth is there was work to be done. I still had to fall flat again and surrender it all to the Lord. A few weeks later, after more counseling and believing Tim was going to turn back to our marriage, I found three letters from the other woman. This time, I saw things differently. This time I saw she had skin in the game and that Tim was in a tug of war—a war between an enemy of our marriage who was playing the sympathetic and supportive role and the good wife who was filled with devastation, pain, anger, and contempt.

The vision I got was of two women holding the ends of a rope, and Tim in the middle, holding on. At one end was a sweet woman saying things like, "I'm so sorry you are having such a hard time. It must be so hard there..." On the other end was me, acting in one of two ways—either like an attacking lion full of hatred for the choices he had made or I was a puddle on the floor that could not stand because of the pain that consumed me. I had to admit that I would rather be at the other end with her than to be with me.

I did not like who I had become. I did not like the contempt I felt, the anger spilling from me, or the pain that held me in bondage.

That vision allowed me to see things differently. As I read the letters to Tim from the other woman over and over, I fell to my knees and surrendered to the Lord. I remember the words I cried: "Take this from me, I can't do this!"

And He did. At that moment, right then, I felt my Father take me in His arms and whisper to me, "I've got you and you will be okay."

With Him, I would be okay. He was all I ever needed. In my journey toward healing, I had surrendered my burden over and over, only to pick it up again and again. This time was different. I could feel His presence and I knew that I was not alone. There was a new assurance that I would be okay, no matter what. God had opened my eyes to the fact that, while I believed in Him, had I ever really trusted Him? Yes, I came to Him in need, but He wanted more. He wanted all of me, and He wanted me to trust Him completely and know that He was enough!

The story doesn't end here. Tim saw a difference in me that day. The reassurance had brought an unexplainable peace to me, one that he saw in my eyes, words, and actions. While he didn't know what had transpired in me that day, he knew he wanted what I had. He wanted to feel that peace that he experienced in me that day. He decided to fight his own battle against the enemies of our marriage and make our marriage work.

Today, we continually celebrate that it is through our Father's grace that we are still standing united, working for His purpose of helping others who are walking through the pain and destruction of betrayal in their marriages. For us it is a privilege and honor to live our lives for God's purpose. He is faithful, and we have been blessed as we walk with other couples through the healing journey of infidelity.

Diana Journy has a passion for helping women find joy and is a Life and Relationship Coach. She is the wife of Tim, mother of four fantastic children, and grandmother to three very special children. Today, Tim and Diana celebrate that through their Father's grace, they are still standing united. Together and separately, they work to help others who are walking through the pain and destruction of betrayal in their relationships and help them to move forward. They consider it a privilege and honor to join their Father in His work. God is faithful and they have been blessed by the doors God has opened for them that have led them to living a life of purpose for His kingdom. Diana is personally grateful that her Heavenly Father walked with her through her pain so that He could use her for His purpose. For her, there is no turning back. To learn more about Diana, visit www.thejourneythrough.com

ROCK BOTTOM IS A BEAUTIFUL PLACE 3

PURSUED BY LOVE

Carlee Liebhart

Surely goodness, mercy and love have hunted me, haunted me, dogged my steps all the days of my life.

– Psalm 23:6 (author's paraphrase)

"I'm leaving you. I've packed everything I want, I've rented an apartment, and I'm leaving—for good! I just want out." These were the words my husband spoke to me at the end of November 2012. My fractured soul was exhausted. I was beyond devastated. But, over a long period of struggling, I had finally accepted his decision to leave and I released him to go. I was resolved to what seemed inevitable. Then in December 2012, right before he planned to move, we received unexpected news that rocked our world and changed the course of both of our lives forever.

Gary was diagnosed with Stage 4 terminal esophageal cancer.

His diagnosis was later changed to advanced instead of terminal because he was so devastated by this news that he wasn't able to process it. He was told to get his affairs in order and that he had less than six to seven months to live.

Whoa, God! No! This has to be a mistake!

Gary was in excellent physical condition, having been a retired Marine and on staff at a local police department. He exercised several times weekly. He was well over six feet tall, and the pure physicality of this man was palpable. This news sent shock waves through me—like being struck by lightning and slammed in the chest by a freight train at the same time. I couldn't believe it! I couldn't breathe. I felt sick to my stomach and caught in a nightmare, wishing someone would please wake me up.

Inside I was screaming and screaming, *No! This is NOT happening!* I was already broken and exhausted from months of marital turmoil, and now I was just confused. I could only imagine how Gary felt, but then a part of me just didn't care. I was filled with so many questions. Who was going to take care of him now? Not me! NOT ME! *Please, please God, not me!* I wanted to wrap my heart in as many protective layers as possible, and shield myself from any more pain. While I had seen the effects of cancer and cancer treatment, it was our relationship (or lack of it) that I struggled so hard against. I was just ready for him to go as he had threatened so many times and leave me in peace. I lay on my face on the floor in the dark that night, broken, confused, exhausted, but still listening. *Comforter, hold me! Hold me!* I was at the end of my rope. I was at Rock Bottom.

Above our mantle is a beautiful picture that says, "In Everything Give Thanks." It was a core belief that would be tested over and over again during the next two years. I didn't feel very thankful. I was petrified and lost in a sea of despair. Gary and I were both a mess! As I lay on the floor that night I whispered, *I love you Father. But, please don't ask this of me.*

I still loved Gary, but didn't believe the relationship was healthy for me anymore. In reality, I was also afraid that if he stayed, I would grow to love him even more and then lose him. I had already lost his love, and I didn't want to risk my heart anymore. I didn't want to be more vulnerable. And yet, I heard my Father's voice gently asking me if I would be willing to put my trust in Him and keep my covenant of marriage, expecting nothing in return. It wasn't a demand...it was a simple question.

Surely God could not ask this of me, not after all that had transpired! Stay with a man who didn't want me? Rejected me? Had even said he didn't want to die with me as his wife? Expect nothing in return? He was leaving me! *Have you lost your mind, God?* Pride...pain...fear...it all whirled inside me, leaving me exposed. I looked and looked for an escape route, anything to avoid what God was asking me to do.

I knew the road ahead would be difficult but, on that fateful day, I made a choice. With tears soaking the carpet, I said, "Yes." Yes, to God's will. Yes, to trusting God. Little did I know then that my amazing and loving Father God was going to take me on a journey of discovery that would irrevocably change my life.

A thought occurred to me, and I got up from the floor and grabbed my journal. I started leafing through the pages and found what I was looking for. In May 2012, just months before his diagnosis, I had written that the Holy Spirit had spoken to me that the Father was going to give me a greater capacity to love. There it was, in writing, a prophetic word of life and hope from my past that I had forgotten about until that moment. Wow!

I thought I already knew about God's love. After all, I'd known Jesus all of my life. I'd heard sermons about being the beloved. My parents were ordained ministers, for heaven's sake! I'd always been a loving person, so what did the Holy Spirit mean by a greater capacity to love? I just didn't get it, but I was about to! I was about to experience a greater revelation of LOVE Himself, the Hound of Heaven who was going to prove relentless in His pursuit of both Gary and me. He loved us so much, that He pursued us even in our brokenness. ESPECIALLY in our brokenness!

I still had expectations, even though the Holy Spirit asked me not to. I thought God would somehow, miraculously, cause us to have this amazing bond and connection as husband and wife again, fighting the big "C" together.

It didn't happen.

Not in the way I expected. Instead, as each day passed, I purposefully and intentionally chose to love my husband. I loved him through obedience and the sacrifice of my service. As the days passed, my heart was filled with compassion. I began to see Gary through the Father's eyes, the way I was seeing myself through our Father's eyes. In the end, it was enough. It was more than enough!

We began the arduous journey of chemotherapy, radiation, and diagnostic test after diagnostic test. Cancer is a relentless disease and cancer centers can be some of the darkest places on the planet. The days turned into weeks and then months. I worked full time, but was allowed to work at home two days weekly. Gary began to isolate himself immediately, so I became his primary caregiver.

On one occasion, I was so tired, I curled into a fetal position. *Do you ever get sick and tired of me being sick and tired, Father?* "Never!" He said. That day I could almost feel His kisses on my face, His breath on my cheek. I had never felt so treasured. I just let Him love on me. My heart was overwhelmed by His loving presence. *What is this love, Father? Consuming my heart with such joy?* Joy is not always an outward expression, but an inward knowing that we are loved, even when we can barely whisper His name. That day, I began to let Him catch me and hold me.

As I walked through the halls of different cancer centers while Gary was in treatment, I had a lot of time on my hands. I was exhausted but couldn't sleep. I began to introduce myself to patients. We often think people are looking for hope when they are sick, but I found they are looking for LOVE. They are love-starved! So, in the midst of all of the chaos, I loved on many families and individuals. I held their hands and touched them and sang to them and cried with them and gave them the love of Jesus Christ through my hands, my tears, and my voice. Why were so many believers love-starved? Had I been love-starved as well and didn't even know it? *I feel such compassion, Father. So many hurting people! Open my eyes to see You, open my ears to hear Your love song. I receive Your love. Show them too!*

Early on in our journey, I knew that Gary would die. I know this is a bold statement. It wasn't a lack of faith—I just knew. This goes against everything I was taught as a believer in the healing power of Jesus Christ. It messed with my head, my heart, and my faith. As you read this, it may mess with yours too. Please, please, if you or a loved one has cancer, this was OUR experience. It was personal and individual. I still believe in healing. In fact, I believe now more than ever in the words of Jesus, "...on earth as it is in Heaven."

The interesting thing is that Gary never asked me to pray for him to be healed of cancer. He asked me for prayer only once. He didn't want to lose his hair. You heard right! I'm still smiling. Gary, my Marine, was meticulous about his appearance. It may seem vain, but I understood. I love my hair too! So I took his beautiful hand in mine and prayed that he would not lose his hair. Through three rounds of the strongest, most wicked chemotherapy, five rounds of radiation and one major surgery, Gary never lost his hair! *You honored his one request, Father.*

Gary was a believer in Christ, but he was petrified of dying. I asked the Holy Spirit how I could help him. It was agonizing watching him suffer physically, but his fear broke my heart. Ten days before he died, I was sitting with him, trying to get him to lie down and go to sleep. He had been up for two days, holding the bars of his bed, refusing to rest. I asked him if he needed to see or talk to someone he had not yet seen. "Do you need to talk to God?" I gently urged him to talk about his fear. Finally, he said he needed to ask for forgiveness for things deep down inside of himself that were hidden. As Gary prayed, he lifted his hands and started to weep and speak in a heavenly language. He had never done this before. The nurse thought he was delusional, but I asked her to leave him in peace. I knew he was lost in the Lord's presence. We cried and worshipped together. It was one of our last conversations and the most sacred moment of our marriage. Then, for the first time in two days, he laid down and slept. *Your goodness and faithfulness overwhelms me! You pursue us with such fierceness and Your love never lets go! I am wrecked!*

I am not a martyr, nor am I a saint for staying with Gary. I am neither. Gary wasn't the "bad guy" because he was leaving me, nor am I the "good" one for staying. Our Father was relentlessly pursuing both of us. He had a plan. He always has a plan! His plan is always His love.

When my Father told me He was going to give me a greater capacity to love, I didn't know it would be so revolutionary. My journey continues to be one of hope, faith, trust, and love. It is about worship in the midst of tragedy. It is about revelation truth concerning God's supernatural love that would transform the way I viewed myself, my God, my husband, and others by transforming the way I saw Him, heard Him, related to Him, and took His love to my world. It is intimate and satisfying, yet leaves me thirsty for more. *I love your presence, Lord!*

I am grateful. Yes, I am. A worshipful heart IS a grateful heart. And worship in the midst of brokenness and suffering is powerful. LOVE revealed Himself to me through this journey. My soul sings! Sometimes it was Papa God holding me in His strong arms, close to His heartbeat, when I was so tired I couldn't even read my Bible, pray, or read my devotional *Jesus Calling*. Sometimes it was the romance and dance of the Lover of my soul who loved on this wife's fractured heart and reminded me who my TRUE husband was. Other times His love was in the sweet caress of the Spirit.

Above my mantle, the "In Everything Give Thanks" picture still hangs. With it is the flag presented to me at Gary's funeral. He was buried with full military honors. The police department escorted our family to the cemetery.

I honor you, Gary. I am thankful we were able to walk this journey together and experience the true meaning of love. I give thanks.

Carlee Liebhart, M.S., is a counselor by vocation, a passionate believer in the goodness of the Father, and a life-long sexual trauma advocate. She has served on the board of a domestic violence shelter and has testified in court trials as a forensic interview expert witness. Carlee is also a Volunteer in Police Service for the police department where her husband retired. During her journey through various cancer centers, she discovered people are both love starved and nutritionally starved due to lack of knowledge. Since her husband's death, she has taken a leap from consumer of It Works! products to distributor. Carlee's passion is to educate others to live a healthy lifestyle for quality of life so they can fulfill their God-given identities, giftings, and destiny. You can contact her through www.carleebow. myitworks.com or beyoubehealthy.blogspot.com

ROCK BOTTOM IS A BEAUTIFUL PLACE 3

EVERYTHING WILL BE OKAY

Brandi Breland-Love

For He will command His angels concerning you, to guard you in all your ways; they will lift you up in their hands, so that you will not strike your foot against a stone.

– Psalm 91:11-12 (NIV)

Rock bottom—what does this phrase really mean? It means the very lowest level, lowest level possible, the absolute bottom.

My lowest level possible is still very fresh in my mind. It was on March 25, 2015. I, like many others, have had a multitude of stressful times in life, different roller coaster rides of emotions and traumatic events that kept me from seeing the light up above. I am a very free-spirited artist, impulsive and creative, while expecting perfection and high achievement in my life. These two things are always at odds with each other, as I'm sure you can imagine. It is a combination of these situations that have led to my seeing multiple psychiatrists and counselors over my lifetime. I've been diagnosed with Severe Depressive Disorder, Major Anxiety Disorder, and ADD over the years. I have also been treated for many different issues, attributing to my physical and mental decline over approximately the last eight years. It was an accumulation of these together that led up to that pivotal day in March.

Looking back, it's surprising that I hadn't hit rock bottom sooner. On that definitive day, I fell to my absolute rock-bottom on the evening of March 25 after a long day of multiple confrontations with family members.

Simply put, I had a nervous breakdown.

Exhausted from the tears that had been flowing for hours, I grabbed my phone and keys, and left the house undetected with no idea where I was going or what was to come. I found myself parked in a lot at one of our parks in town. As I watched the families having a great time and saw the children playing, I continued to cry uncontrollably. It was in that moment I realized that I was helpless, hopeless, and ultimately faithless. That last string of faith in my heart, the one I was always so proud to have, had finally broken. While my mind and thoughts were reeling out of control, I was able to recognize the passive suicidal thoughts I was experiencing.

Scared out of my mind, I frantically searched on my phone for the nearest hospital or hotline.

I was right in the middle of my manic episode with no results from my frantic search, but God sent an angel in the form of a simple phone call. That call was from my little love, Mercey. She's my youngest, about to start her senior year in high school.

Now, I can't deny that I hesitated to answer her call because I did not want her to know that I was losing myself to the deep abyss I was in. However, at the last minute, I thought to myself, "I must answer, because she will be worried about me if I don't." I absolutely know she was my guardian angel sent from Heaven above, to save me from myself that terrible night.

When I finally answered the phone, she questioned my leaving without saying goodbye, which was very out of character for me. I answered her as best I knew how, being completely honest. I told her I thought I needed to go to the hospital. She pleaded with me to go to a friend's house, and I promised, I actually promised her, that I would. Somehow I ended up at a friend's apartment and the rest of the night is mainly just a blur. I do remember once I got back home, my sweet Mercey and my husband Kyle were there to help me through the night. The next morning, after Kyle spoke with my psychiatrist, I said goodbye to Mercey and went with him to be admitted into the psychiatric hospital.

The next two weeks were the most eye-opening, and at the same time hardest, most confusing times that I've ever experienced. My diagnoses? Bipolar disorder accompanied with the major depressive disorder and severe anxiety disorder. As you might imagine, my thoughts in the beginning went something like this: *Bipolar? No way! Only crazy and really sick people have bipolar disorder.* However, during my stay, I learned how wrong those stigmas are. As I began to dissect my past, it became apparent to me that I most certainly was bipolar. Still, to this day, I am continuing to learn about bipolar disorder and how it affects me, as well as the effects it has on family and friends.

During my hospital stay, the Lord showed me just how precious my guardian angel, Mercey, was. She visited me everyday, sometimes twice a day. She was already learning about my bipolar disorder and began helping me to understand it for myself. When I would have some negative episodes while she was around, she would help me to calm myself. I am so grateful that God sent her to my rescue that deep dark night in March. As I and others worked through our pain, it helped me to realize I was not alone in my struggles. I was able to see what most doctors over the years had disregarded with, "It's all in your head. You're just depressed. Here take this pill," was a gross misdiagnosis, and I was feeling out of control for a real reason.

I came to realize my spiritual gift of caretaker had become my greatest weakness. All of my life, I've used my gift to focus on helping others before helping myself. I am known as the best listener and advisor for others. I always put others before myself because that is what makes me feel amazing in my heart. I am always losing myself in the call of help from others. In the past, I lived my life as the most tolerant best friend for many people who abused my friendship in different ways.

My other gift is forgiving others with an unconditional love. I was always trying to help them through whatever struggles they were experiencing, again losing myself in the process. This gift became my weakness as well because I did not know how to ask for help. I would rather hide and just overlook my own needs.

By the time I hit my rock bottom, I had no idea who Brandi was. I was so good at hiding myself in others that no one knew I needed help. As a result of my hopeless experience, I have learned to focus on my needs as well. I'm recognizing that I am perfect in His eyes and that my self-goals of perfection must change. I am learning to listen to my body and my mind. I have to live minute by minute and set smaller daily goals for myself that are attainable. This experience has changed me in many other ways, but most importantly, it has brought me closer to the Lord. I am seeking His guidance through this healing process and trusting in Him once more. I struggle daily with giving things up to Him and taking them right back, trying to fix them myself. However, I am working on it.

Roses and butterflies have always symbolized so much for me. Roses represent unconditional love and beauty to me, and this feeling began when I was about seventeen. Everyone sees the rose as a delicate flower protected by its prickly thorns. I agree with this perception, however, I feel a much deeper connection. My sweet grandma loved roses, and passed that love to me. Just like a rose reaches for the sky to grow and live on, I see myself reaching towards the heavens to grow and repair my heart. A passion for butterflies has risen out of my love for my beautiful children and their many journeys through life. I see them as caterpillars in their cocoon, learning and growing as young children, and maturing to fly free and reach for amazing heights. Now I, too, feel like I am a butterfly in a cocoon. I am developing and growing in Christ, learning to find myself, and as my little love so eloquently put it, knowing everything will be okay. I must continue learning to lean on Him, trust myself, and to ask my family and friends for help when I need it and not when it is too late. I do believe that when I am ready, I will fly to heights unknown.

Today I reflect back on my life and feel I have surpassed the dark abyss of my rock-bottom experience. However, I am still working daily to stay on the uphill track, to ask for help when it is needed, to not judge myself, and to give myself attainable, smaller goals to help me feel confident in myself. Although I am still surrounded by many external challenging circumstances, all of which I have no control over, I must move forward and especially lean on others for support and help. I have learned that I must do all of this, for it's by practicing these skills, and striving to strengthen and grow in my faith, that I will reach a place of peace and tranquility in my journey through life.

Psalm 40: 2-3

He brought me up out of the pit of destruction, out of the miry clay,

And He set my feet upon a rock making my footsteps firm.

He put a new song in my mouth, a song of praise to our God;

Many will see and fear

And will trust in the Lord.

Brandi Love is a native Texan currently residing in Round Rock. She was given a new lease on life on June 4, 2005 when she married her high school best friend, Kyle. Together they have three beautiful children: Garrett, Lauren, and Mercey. Brandi graduated from Midwestern State University with a Fine Arts Degree and is the owner of LENZ Photography. Her faith and family have always been her passion in life. After relocating and working a "real" job for the last few years, she is re-branding and moving forward in faith to launch her photography business. She is also excited about the opportunity to enter the fine art world of gallery exhibits for ceramics and paintings. While still in the middle of her journey, she is passionately pursuing God's will for her life and seeking the balance that we all desire in our daily walk. You can reach Brandi at brandi@lenz.photography.

A WHISPER IN
THE WHIRLWIND

Hanne Moon

Furthermore, we know that God causes everything to work together for the good of those who love God...

– Romans 8:28

Sometimes when God speaks to you, it's a quiet whisper in your spirit. At other times, it's a barely audible voice that has you checking to see who else is in the room. And sometimes it's a disquiet so profound that only in hindsight do you recognize the Master's voice.

This story begins with my childhood. Being a military brat meant moving...a lot. Between my father's tours overseas and several stateside stations, I went to seventeen different schools before graduating. We plucked up and moved constantly, once three times in one school year. It was hard to make friends, and it was hard to keep them. Promises to stay in touch soon faded with yet another school and attempts to fit in.

I won't lie—while I loved the different cultures and things to do and see, part of me longed for stability. I didn't know what it felt like to have the continuity of friends, family, and community that one grew up in. I barely knew my aunts, uncles or cousins. I can't Facebook those friends that I've had since grade school. Distance has been more than the space between two places on the map. It has been a distance of the heart as well.

By the time the end of my junior year arrived, my father had retired from the military, had tried to partner in a business with his sister and brother-in-law (which fell through within a year), and soon moved back to his Mississippi hometown with a job with the post office. We moved with him during the last six weeks of my junior year. I was the new girl for the last six weeks of school and pretty much alone throughout the summer.

My senior year started off with a bang. I made friends, had loads of fun, and finally began to feel a part of something, a part of a community. I had church friends and school friends. We played jokes on each other, stuffed ourselves into cars until the doors bulged, and danced to the Commodores at the homecoming game.

For once, I felt normal.

I was determined to make this town my home. I was through moving. Even though I was only sixteen when I began college, I knew that I had had enough adventure to last a lifetime. It was time to settle down. And that's what I did. I went to school, took a job, got an apartment, fell in love, and married. We worked and we started to raise our family. And then life intervened.

General Motors closed the plant my husband worked at. We had three choices—he could retire before he had his mandatory thirty years (he had twenty) and try to find another job that paid as well, we could become GM gypsies, or he could try to commute on the weekends from the plant he was being transferred to.

We tried the commute.

It didn't work.

Mandatory overtime kept him away from home, and when he did come home for a weekend, he was exhausted. The drive didn't seem worth the trouble. I knew that I was going to have to make a decision about selling the house and moving with him.

To say that I railed against this would be an understatement. I yelled at God. I screamed at Him and I cried. We had just finished building the house we lived in. It was the first permanent place I had called home and was barely five years old. It was the only place that had ever been mine. I had put a lot of time and energy into the house, staining every wood surface and painting every wall. My children had hopscotch squares under the carpet where they had played hopscotch on the concrete slab as we finished the wiring, plumbing, Sheetrock and finish work.

I didn't understand—everyone else had permanence. Why couldn't I? But that Christmas, as we opened presents and I looked into the weary eyes of my husband, I told him I'd begin packing. I said I'd rather we lived in a cardboard box together than apart another minute. We took the next few weeks shoving everything into boxes, and I said goodbye to the only house that I had ever loved. I didn't do it with a willing heart however. I was still seething at God for what I perceived as His capriciousness in my life.

⟡

The girls were growing and after the first few months, had adjusted to Tuscaloosa and their new school and friends. My youngest, Nikki, was fourteen. As she hit her teenage years, she began experiencing what I perceived to be migraine headaches, though they were somewhat unusual. I had migraines and was aware they ran in families. The headaches were infrequent at first, and I honestly didn't think much about them except to provide her the same homeopathic remedies I was using.

One day she came home with a brochure from a missions group in Texas. She wanted to go on a missions outreach to Thailand and said she would raise the money herself. She began having bake sales, selling Popsicles, having car washes, and working for the money for her trip. She was very successful at her fundraising and eventually raised enough money to go. We packed her luggage, and took her to Tyler, Texas.

On the six-hour trip back home, I received a phone call. It was Nikki, and she seemed about to cry. She said that she was having some difficulties and that she wasn't sure she wanted to go. These difficulties were more religious-based than physical at the time. She was used to a more conservative, sedate faith. The boisterous faith of the missions group was unnerving to her. I told her she had several days of intake and training for the trip. If she decided she definitely didn't want to go, she was to call me and I'd come for her. She seemed to feel better after our talk, agreed to stay, and hung up the phone.

I hadn't been home an hour when the phone rang again. It was Nikki. They had taken her to the hospital and the doctor decided she was dehydrated. When she got on the phone, she told me she wasn't dehydrated and they wouldn't listen to her. She said she had become short of breath, excessively so, and her heart had begun beating heavily. They insisted on beginning an IV, and she was scared.

We lived on a small homestead at the time and had eleven horses. We baled and gathered hay as a family in the heat of the Deep South. We mucked out stalls and tended to horses in 100-degree weather. My daughter was athletic in nature and knew what it meant to be dehydrated. When she told me she wasn't, I believed her. My husband and I both talked to her and the person in charge, and we said we'd be heading back to Texas immediately.

We made the trip at breakneck speed, garnering a speeding ticket in Louisiana in the process. When we arrived at the facility in Texas, Nikki had decided by that time that she wasn't making the trip after all. We gathered her belongings and brought her back home. Everything seemed to return to normal. She said her breathing was fine and she felt great. I began to wonder if she hadn't suffered some sort of panic attack in unfamiliar surroundings.

Then, a few days later, as she stood at the stove cooking some breakfast, she suddenly grabbed her head, staggered, and nearly fell down. My husband and I jumped up and asked her what had happened, and she said she had felt a lightning bolt of pain go through her head. She shook her head and said she was fine, just a little dizzy.

I immediately called a neurologist I knew and made her an appointment. If these were migraines, they were no longer presenting like any I had ever experienced before.

The neurologist was a wonderful Christian doctor and the most amazing diagnostician I had ever encountered. He was patient and kind with Nikki, and after spending about an hour with us, ordered MRIs and x-rays. He set an appointment for the next week to discuss his findings.

That next week we were introduced to the term "Chiari malformation," a genetic anomaly of the skull and brain stem. The brain sits too low in the skull, and the skull and spine put pressure on the brain and spinal column. It can cause severe debilitation and disability. He said we needed to see a neurosurgeon and that we were probably looking at surgery to correct the problem.

The doctor we took her to couldn't establish a rapport with my daughter. Nikki was pensive and very closed-mouth in his office. Without Nikki's input (and he refused to listen to mine), the surgeon could only rely on the films, and he said if it were his daughter, he'd wait a year before deciding on surgery. He said she was growing, and that it was premature to make a decision for such drastic surgery at the time. He didn't feel like there was any immediate health concerns.

I lay in bed that night, replaying the scene at the doctor's office over and over in my mind. My husband was relieved with the diagnosis, but I was unsettled and ill at ease in my spirit. It was a feeling I couldn't explain. I felt this urgent nudge to get a second opinion. I wondered if my fears were playing havoc with me, but that quiet inner voice would not be silenced. The next morning, I called the original neurologist's office to discuss the surgeon's findings.

I was told emphatically that I did need a second opinion, and their office would set me an appointment with another doctor well-versed in the Chiari syndrome. They made us an appointment with Children's Hospital in Birmingham. Two days later, we were navigating a labyrinth of corridors that seemed to go on forever and in no particular direction.

I filled out insurance forms, medical history forms, and all types of paperwork, and then Nikki and I sat and waited for what seemed an eternity. The receptionist called our name, asked for the MRIs I was carrying, and told us it would be a while before the doctor could see us.

We sat and made plans for the rest of the day—lunch, shopping, and the bookstore. The next forty-five minutes were spent discussing the newest fashions, how hungry we were, and the latest guy she was head over heels for.

Mothers with children in wheelchairs and obvious neurological problems surrounded me. These children couldn't talk, had to have assistance breathing, and endured spastic limbs and tics. I breathed several prayers for these people, as well as a prayer of thanksgiving for the health of my family.

I felt foolish for insisting we come here.

My daughter didn't belong in this place.

Our name was called, and we were ushered into a room. A round of residents and interns came in and spoke with Nikki, asking dozens of questions. They assured me the doctor would be in shortly.

After about twenty minutes, the doctor strode into the room. He was a professor at UAB and in charge of pediatric neurosurgery. He was a no-nonsense type of man, slightly imperious in nature, but obviously competent.

He jammed the MRIs into the light box and sat down on a roll-around stool. He grabbed a long swab, told Nikki to open her mouth, and proceeded to poke her tongue, the roof of her mouth, and the back of her throat. He looked at the x-rays one more time then turned to me.

"Your daughter needs surgery, and she needs it today."

I stared at him, my mouth gaping. Nikki and I glanced at each other, and I turned with a puzzled frown back to the doctor. It was taking me a few moments to process what he was saying. I had gone from "let's wait a year" to "today."

"Your daughter will be dead in six months, Mrs. Moon." I can't define the ice that settled into my belly at those words. I was in shock and could only sit and listen as he tried to explain why he was so adamant about the surgery being done as quickly as possible. He pointed out the areas of compression she was experiencing on her brain stem, how her gag reflex was non-existent, and that her breathing would be the next thing to go.

Suddenly, the symptoms she had experienced in Texas made sense. "I'll clear my schedule and we'll do the surgery in the morning," the doctor said, interrupting my thoughts. With that, he walked out of the room, leaving me with a stream of nurses and receptionists as we made arrangements to admit Nikki to the hospital.

I don't remember much of the next twenty-four hours. It's a blur. But in the time after her surgery, before she woke up, I put aside my foolish quarrel with God and asked Him to please look after her. I asked Him for her health and her safety. I asked Him to do one of two things: either heal her completely or take her home. We had dire predictions of paralysis and possible brain damage. I didn't want this vibrant sweet child to experience that.

Despite those predictions, Nikki recovered one hundred percent. She is healthy and active, married, with two children of her own. She now teaches at the same school she graduated from.

But in the aftermath of her surgery and after she came home to recover, I finally relaxed and allowed myself some extra time to spend with the Father. I thanked Him for my blessings and my daughter's life. I tabled my quarrel. I wouldn't bring it up again.

God had other plans. *Do you see now why I had you move?*

My thoughts went still. Had I heard right?

Which doctor in your Mississippi town would you have taken her to for this?

And I knew the answer immediately—there was no one. We would have treated it as migraines until it was too late.

Do you doubt that I know what you will need, even years into the future?

The tears began. "No doubt, Father...there is no doubt."

I have learned to live with a grateful heart from that moment on. Even when I don't understand the reasons that things happen, I have no doubt that my Father understands and has a plan to use it for good. That doesn't mean I don't have moments when I question—we all do! What it means is that I have learned to turn those doubts into praise because God has proven that He is able to take care of our souls and our lives.

Sometimes our Father's voice is a whisper on the wind, or clarity of thought when reading a passage of scripture.

Sometimes it's a prodding, insistent reverberation deep in our souls, compelling us to obey.

Whichever way He chooses to manifest Himself to me in the future, I never want to be in a position where I might mistake that Voice again.

Hanne Moon is a freelance writer, editor, and independent publisher of quality non-fiction and fiction through her publishing company Heritage Press Publications. She has an avid love of the written word and enjoys helping writers find their voices. A self-confessed book addict, chocolate lover, coffee snob, and Jesus follower, Hanne divides her time between work, family life, her vegetable garden, chickens, dogs, and grandchildren, all on 27 acres in Mississippi.

LOST, BUT NOW FOUND

Ronda Neufeld

"For I know the plans I have for you," says the Lord. "they are plans for good and not for disaster, to give you a future and a hope. In those days when you pray, I will listen. If you look for me wholeheartedly, you will find me."

– Jeremiah 29:11-13 (NLT)

Isn't it interesting how some events become crystal clear memories that remain forever emblazoned in our minds?

I remember that early morning flight en route to Florida. I was flying south to be a member of a marriage seminar team. It was my first seminar in the role of a mentor instead of a participant. But I was going alone. My husband Barry was unable to attend with me due to work obligations. I was excited, apprehensive, and anxious.

The first leg of the journey from Calgary to Dallas was four hours. I remember the crispness of the early morning air. There was a sleepy stillness in the airplane cabin. The plane was not full and for some reason, I had a whole row to myself. I had space—and solitude! I had the sense of embarking on an adventure! I reached into my travel bag and took out the beautiful new leather journal that my husband had given to me as a gift. I had been waiting for a special occasion to make the first pen strokes, and this was it. Crisp pages...waiting.

I began writing, in the form of a prayer. I thanked God for the journey He had travelled with me...for healing me. I wrote these words.

> *Thank you for the peace and healing you have brought into my life. Thank you that you redeem. Thank you for your love that knows no bounds. "Make me an instrument of your love." These words come to me...it is what I desire, and yet I no longer quickly embrace them because I know how tools are made—how they are forged, fired, and hammered!! Oh, the forging is hard!! The master blacksmith you are, GOD. It is not an easy task for You or ME. Am I the sword you can use yet? Have I braved the fire? Am I ready to face the task?*

Then the tears began! For almost four hours I sobbed and wept. The forging had nearly cost me my family—and my life. I grieved over the memories that were now part of my story. And I shed tears in awe and gratitude for God's faithful presence in my life.

I remembered a night almost three years before, walking along the creek. It was a dreary, gray rainy night. I remember sobbing and weeping then too. I knew I couldn't continue life as I had been living. I had to make a decision to leave my family or leave the thing (I thought) that had given me new hope. I was crying out to God in my brokenness and despair. I remember feeling a strange sensation of a presence by my shoulder. And then the words, *It will be okay.* What? Again, *It will be okay.* That statement was an utter impossibility for me in that moment.

I was in my early forties and LOST. I had been married for twenty-two years to the man I loved and believed God intended for me. We married in the glow of the belief that we would go to the mission field or do some big thing for God. Our family grew with the births of two beautiful, healthy, and active sons.

We had a busy life. Both boys were involved in high-level competitive sport and we travelled with them a lot. A LOT. We were busy. Too busy. I had been primarily a stay-at-home mom, occasionally working part-time, but now I had just bought a new business. It was something to give me purpose. My life had the appearance of being good. Some parts of it were good. But *I* was not.

I was lost, depressed and drifting.

A year earlier I had travelled overseas with one of my sons. He had been invited to participate with a group of Canadian kids in an international sports program. I was experiencing significant struggles with clinical depression in this season of my life. I felt I was barely hanging on. It was during this time—away from home, in a foreign environment—that my world changed.

It was not anything I ever had anticipated or looked for. But I was vulnerable...and someone was kind to me. I noticed, and I felt noticed. Another broken soul—looking.

A shock rang through my system, shouting in the fog of my mind—I mattered!! Over the years, in the busy-ness of life, somehow I had lost ME. I played a myriad of roles with success. I was a devoted mom and a committed wife.

But that was the problem—I was somebody's mom, somebody's wife, somebody's daughter or daughter-in-law. I was a character in everyone else's lives and I had ceased to exist. Now this spark happened and suddenly, I was important because he saw ME. And I made the decision to compromise all that I had built my life on and for, all that I loved and held most dear to my heart. I stepped outside my marriage.

I traded it all to feel noticed.

While there was excitement and hope, another part of me plunged into deep guilt and unrelenting shame. Still, I could not let go. When I returned home, blame and anger became my defensive walls toward everyone, especially my husband. I justified my choices. The affair became my answer, and I did not let go. The spiral of deceit and despair continued its downward journey.

I remember sitting at the supper table one night, the conflict in my heart manifesting as physical pain so intense I could barely breathe. I looked at my beautiful beloved sons, knowing I would destroy them if I left...

And feeling that I would die if I stayed. Still I could not let go.

But God was with me through it all. When I thought I hit rock bottom that night in the rain, feeling like I could no longer go on, I felt His presence and I heard Him say, *It will be okay.* I did not understand what that meant. How could anything ever be okay again?

Being "okay" was the incomprehensible work of God's mercy when a week later my husband picked up my phone and found text messages from another man. Real solid rock bottom had arrived.

In the beauty of God's amazing grace, it also meant that healing could now begin. It meant that God could now make this crooked path straight once more. It meant that the lies would now face truth, and the light could now come and reveal what the darkness hid.

Agonizing months of pain and insanity followed. Betrayal causes pain beyond belief. All affair discoveries are horrible. Ours was no different. Everyone was told—my sons, my family, my business partner, the sports parents. As is often the case, the chaos had financial repercussions, and we felt that bitter sting. Pain that came from breaking innocent trust settled in my sons' hearts. My brokenness and shame seemed to never end. I attempted to end my life twice. But ALWAYS, God was with me.

He had a plan for my husband and me when we did not have strength to eat or energy to close our eyes at night. He was with us...ALWAYS.

Soon after disclosure, we were given the opportunity to attend a personal development seminar called CHOICES (thank you, Thelma Box, for the work of your heart!). It was a difficult week in our state of marital crisis, but it was divine timing for me. CHOICES saved me from the faded woman I had become. I came away believing I was a strong woman, that I could survive this. It was the mantra that helped me put my feet on the ground each morning. They were the words that helped me face my shame.

Several months later, we attended a marriage seminar that dealt with infidelity. We met other couples with unique story lines, but always the story of betrayal was the same—heart-rending devastation for both the betrayed and the unfaithful. That weekend, in the midst of all the pain in the room, our marriage was saved.

Healing was a long road. Broken trust had to be rebuilt. New patterns had to be developed. I take full responsibility for the decisions I made and the consequences that followed, but we both acknowledge that we had dysfunction in our marriage pre-affair. Faulty foundations had to be torn down so that a healthy, whole, healed relationship could become possible. It was a long road.

This is the amazing thing, and the thing that I am most grateful for—in the midst of it all, I found ME!! I AM a strong and WORTHY woman. And God has a call on my life.

This woman was strong enough to board that early morning flight to Florida. She was strong enough to face twenty-five couples caught in the snare of infidelity, as a woman who had been unfaithful!! Let me tell you about relying on God and reaching into deep places for strength! This is the truth of what God spoke to me—I was a vessel forged in fire, designed to carry hope for those broken lives, families, and homes.

My husband and I now work as marriage coaches. We specialize in working with couples dealing with affair recovery. In the months following affair disclosure, life can be best described as insanity. We believe that the healing in our lives enables us to sit with couples in the midst of their storm because we have overcome this treacherous path. We have hope and peace to offer, and tools to help survive the devastation. We can be one place of solace and solidness that they can lean on when the rest of life has turned upside down.

There are times when I still grieve for the lost woman I was and the devastating choices I made. I wish that this story was not a part of my story. I wish I could make the consequences disappear. But then I remember the full measure of God's redeeming love and healing power. I walk daily in the knowledge that He calls me a WORTHY woman. Every day I choose to live as that woman, the woman who is loved beyond belief by Father GOD!! I am never out of His favored sight. And regardless of what happens in my world, I am always the apple of my Heavenly Father's eyes. My rock bottom is the place where truth collided with my life and God met me. Rock bottom is the source of the strength I share with the world.

This is the rest of the journal entry on that flight to Dallas in the aftermath of the tears.

January 28

Make me a vessel of your healing God. I am the vessel that you have created—I am the vessel that you have formed. I am a container that carries your restoration. But I am only the vessel. Healing cannot flow from an empty cup. Cleanse the vessel— cleanse me. Then fill me. Fill me with your healing waters. Let the vessel be ready to release the healing flood. May your mercy be extended to the children you love. May YOUR words flow—not mine. I am happy to be the vessel, the container through which your love moves. Because this is what you created me to be! I am the vessel—YOU are the flood.

Ronda Neufeld is a life and relationship coach, a (some days) retired florist, and budding photographer. She recently founded Cherished Heart Community, a gathering of women who have tasted the storms of life and know of its challenges, but are making choices to live with radiant hearts and clear vision. Follow the journey on Facebook—Cherished Heart Community or visit rondaneufeld.com. Ronda and her loving husband (whom she loves with all her heart!) coach couples and individuals through relationship and marriage crisis. They feel a deep calling to work with couples dealing with infidelity. If you or someone you know needs help walking through this pain, please contact them through the website rondaneufeld.com.

ROCK BOTTOM IS A BEAUTIFUL PLACE 3

THE BOOKENDS
OF LIFE

Terri Schrews

*Everything will be all right in the end...if it's not all right
then it's not yet the end.*

– Deborah Moggach, *The Best Exotic Marigold Hotel*

After my youngest daughter was born, I had a really hard time bouncing
back. I always struggled with my pregnancies and was slow to bounce
back in general, but this time was especially difficult—even for me. I
was tired all the time, fatigued to the point I struggled to make it through
the day. I was experiencing weird pain, random fevers, body aches,

and occasional numbness in my hands and feet. It felt something like a lingering case of the flu that just wouldn't let up. Finally, after about six months, I decided I needed to see someone, so I made an appointment with my family doctor.

My doctor asked the routine questions, took some blood, and ordered a series of tests. A week or so later when he called with the results, there was not much in the way of answers. Low vitamin D, some other labs that seemed sort of off, nothing that stood out as really out of the ordinary. He suggested I take a couple of supplements and give it a little more time, that perhaps it was a postpartum issue.

Over the next several months, it became clear something more was going on. Annoying fatigue became crippling exhaustion. Uncomfortable aches turned into swollen and intensely painful joints. My body was doing strange things. It was out of whack. Unable to shake it (yes, I spent weeks telling myself I could), I finally called the doctor again.

The second medical appointment was different than the first. Many of my joints were red and obviously swollen. My heartbeat was fast, and my blood pressure would drop off suddenly without warning—usually upon standing or changing positions. I had more outward symptoms than I had months earlier. More tests were ordered, different tests than the first time. There was one question that stood out though. During the exam, my doctor asked if I had been bitten by a tick.

When I left the office, I immediately called my husband to talk about the appointment. We both laughed when I told him the doctor asked if I had been bitten by a tick. That may seem odd, but truthfully, I wasn't sure I had ever even seen a tick, let alone been bitten by one. We live in the suburbs, and I am not exactly what you would call the outdoorsy type and I've never been camping. It seemed so far-fetched that we joked that if I had Lyme disease, everyone must have it.

Almost two weeks passed before I got the results of all my tests. I was completely stunned by the diagnosis. In what seemed like a surreal twist of fate, I was told I had indeed tested positive for Lyme disease. At first I didn't believe it, was certain it had to be a mistake, but I was quickly assured there was no mistake. As confusing as it was, I also felt a sense of relief because I was assured it was not going to be a big deal.

Fourteen days of antibiotics and I would be good as new. I think that's true for some people. It wasn't true for me. My symptoms only intensified with the first round of antibiotics. After a month, my doctor placed me on an additional round of antibiotics, another thirty days of treatment. Sixty days into the diagnosis, I could barely get out of bed.

To make matters worse, my doctor seemed to be out of solutions. He said I should be fine, but I wasn't anywhere in the vicinity of fine. I didn't know where to turn. I was sick, deathly sick, and my life was falling apart.

Lyme disease is a weird and baffling illness, surrounded by huge medical controversy. Some doctors believe it is merely a short-term infection, quickly cleared by short-term antibiotics. Others believe it is the root cause for many chronic diseases and conditions ranging from multiple sclerosis, to Parkinson's disease, and more. Personally, I would have preferred not to find myself in the middle of it, but that is right where I was.

It was so humbling. Self-reliant, independent, overcomer—these were words I had come to identify with in my life. Finding myself in a place where I was unable to run my business, earn a living, or care for the needs of my family shook me to the core.

Deep questions of self-worth and value plagued me. Would I ever be well again? Is a life spent in a dark room in pain and misery worth living? Didn't my husband deserve a partner he could enjoy life with? What about my children? They needed a mother who could be present and involved! I was desperate for help. I just wanted to be well, to find some answers.

My search for health included a host of medical professionals. There was a "Lyme literate MD," a neurologist, rheumatologist, an internist, a sleep specialist, chiropractor, cardiologist, and an infectious disease doctor. Each one had a differing opinion. The only thing they seemed to agree on was the fact they disagreed. They disagreed about the diagnosis, they disagreed about the science, and they disagreed about the treatment.

After a while, I stopped mentioning Lyme disease at all. I was afraid to even bring it up because there was so much shaming from the mainstream medical community. They offered alternative explanations: fibromyalgia, inflammatory arthritis, and others.

For more than a year and a half, I was fed a steady stream of medications. Massive amounts of antibiotics, pills to keep me alert, another to put me to sleep, pills for inflammation, muscle spasms, pain, depression—there were so many pills. I asked repeatedly if it was okay to take them all. Each time I was assured it was not uncommon. The benefits outweighed the risks, I was told.

Sometimes, it felt like the medications were helping. Other times, I felt I could no longer tell the difference between side effects and symptoms. The entire turn of events was so confusing, and I still didn't even know with absolute certainty exactly what was wrong. I guess the answer depended on who you asked—and each doctor was convinced he or she was the right one. While I didn't know it yet, I was about to plunge into a downward spiral that would feel much like hell on earth.

I had been sick for a long time, but something different had begun happening. My heart raced all the time it seemed. The simple act of breathing had become a chore. My head felt like it was literally going to explode and my muscles would twitch uncontrollably. I blacked out at times. I knew something was very wrong, and though I didn't express it to anyone, I began to fear it might be the end. I thought I might die.

During a particularly difficult evening, I made an emergency appointment with my neurologist. I was afraid to go, that I wouldn't be taken seriously, but I didn't know what else to do. The next day, my husband Mark helped me dress and gently loaded me into the car for yet one more appointment. As we sat in the waiting room, I prayed a quiet, desperate prayer. *Lord, please give this doctor wisdom. Please help me.*

When they called me back, I had to cling to Mark's arm to keep from fainting. My head was spinning. I'll never forget what happened next. The doctor came in, sat down across from me, and very gently started to speak. He said, "Your heartbeat is really elevated. Why are you so anxious?" Then he said, "I'm not trying to hurt you, but I really think you should consider seeing a psychiatrist."

There were more words after that, but I didn't hear them. The tears just flowed down my face. I couldn't stop them. Was this the wisdom from God I had prayed for? In my heart of hearts, I knew something else was wrong, but no one would believe me. My doctors thought I was mentally ill—at least some of them anyway. Maybe they were right. Maybe I was a hypochondriac. I had lost my mind and my body had gone along for the ride. I felt as if no part of my former life was left. No dignity, no meaning, nothing.

Later that night, I sat on the stairs of my home and prayed. I cried and I prayed. "Lord God, if I have a mental illness, then I am willing to accept that. Just please, please, help me get help." At the time, I thought I was at my rock bottom, but it was still to come.

Within days I was in the hospital. Most of what happened that week is still a blur. I remember pieces of conversations here and there. Things said in the midst of days of darkness. At one point, a nurse said to another, "I cannot take care of her. She keeps rambling and getting up and falling out of the bed. I wish they would just move her to intensive care." I was there, but without a voice. Present, but just existing.

This right here, this was my rock bottom, and it was swimming in a sea of shame.

No longer was I a respected member of the community, successful businesswoman, and loving wife and mother. I was the patient. The patient who had a break with reality and was convinced she had some kind of crippling disease. Psychiatric medication, that was the next pill added to the mix.

There are two passages of scripture I consider to be like the bookends of my life. The first is Romans 8:1: "Therefore, there is now no condemnation for those who are in Christ Jesus" (NIV). The second is John 10:10: "The thief comes only to steal, kill, and destroy. I came that they may have life and have it abundantly" (ESV). I refer to these verses as bookends because the first reminds me of who I am, and the second reminds me of what Christ died to give me. The whole of everything else fits inside these unwavering truths.

In the darkness of my life, I had forgotten this.

And He reminded me.

Each afternoon, a lovely Caribbean woman would come into my room to mop the floors and take out the trash. On the third day, she closed the door behind her when she came in. Silently, she came over to the side of my bed and sat down. Then she gently placed her hands on my head and began to pray. She spoke life back into my broken heart, saying, "My dear you have not been given a spirit of fear. You have a sound mind. What the doctors say, it is not true. You are blessed and chosen of God." She stayed awhile, just holding my hands and praying so softly I couldn't hear her. I'm not even sure when she left.

The next morning when the doctor came in, he said I needed to stop taking several of the medications I had been on, including the ones he had recently added. When I entered the hospital, I was carrying a Ziploc bag with almost a dozen prescriptions in it. They kept giving them to me. As it turns out, the pills *were* the problem. I had serotonin syndrome, which is a dangerous and potentially fatal drug interaction caused by the combination of prescriptions. I had likely been experiencing problems related to these drug interactions for months.

Though my rock bottom was a scary and dangerous place, it is also a beautiful place. It's a beautiful place because in my darkest moments, I learned more than I ever could have otherwise about the depths of God's love for me. Not only did He save my life and reveal the source of the problem, He also sent someone to sit by my side and tell me the shame was not mine. That woman put her job at risk in order to be obedient to what God called her to do—and she did it for a total stranger. How can I be anything but grateful?

Our Father always knows what we need to hear, and His message is always right on time...

There is no condemnation for those who are in Christ Jesus.

I have come to accept I am never going to have all the answers to the questions I have about those years I lost to illness, and that's okay. God has healed me. He has brought healing to my physical body, to my spirit, and to my emotions, which took such a beating...

I came that they may have life and have it abundantly.

Today, I live with a grateful heart because I know God is who He says He is, and He will do what He has promised to do. He works all things for our good.

And if it's not good yet, it's not the end.

Terri Schrews is a professional life coach and full-time realtor. A long-time entrepreneur, she is passionate about helping others move forward in the direction of their dreams. Over the course of her career, Terri has owned a nationally franchised real estate company, started a coaching practice, sold lipstick, succeeded much, failed often, and kept on going. Her heartbeat is inspiring women to live courageously so they may create more authentic, rewarding, and purpose-filled lives. Learn more at www.TerriSchrews.com

FINDING THE SILVER LINING

Marsha Sherrill

The light shines in the darkness, and the darkness can never extinguish it.

– John 1:5 (NLT)

Shortly after waking up each morning, I take a few minutes out to write in my gratitude journal. I have been writing in a gratitude journal off and on for several years. It is a journal that is separate from my main journal. Sometimes there are long entries, but many times they are short. Some days I don't feel like being grateful. On those days, which I call my "temper tantrum days," I sit for a while and write something anyway, whether I feel like it or not. There is always something in my life to be grateful for. The one thing that is obvious is that I woke up!

Prior to getting clean and sober, gratitude and humility were not obvious priorities in my life. There were certainly occasions where I would be grateful for a situation or someone doing something for me, but as a way of life, no way. Being grateful is a lifestyle. I have come to believe gratitude and humility are close relatives.

My road to gratitude was not a quick and easy process. Gratitude developed over time, with maturity, through hard times and dark days. It was easy to be grateful when life was smooth and things were going my way—engulfed in love, bills paid, no drama, serenity abounding, healthy body, sunshine everywhere I went. I felt as though I had the Midas touch.

Then there were those times when money was short, and I thought for sure I would end up homeless or in the soup line; or the time when my mammogram came back questionable and I had to have a biopsy; when the guy I was in a relationship with decided it was cool to sleep around and afterwards tell me about it; or another situation where the guy chose dope over me.

It was during these times where I had to dig deep for something to be grateful for. My hurt and fear ran deep. I could not see the sun shining because of the darkness. One thing for sure, each of these situations kept me in prayer. I prayed for relief from what I was feeling. I prayed for God to resolve the problem with the results I wanted. I did not know yet about asking for strength to get through the darkness.

One of the biggest lessons I learned about gratitude is trust. Yep, trust. Trusting the process. Sometimes things happen in life that we don't like or agree with. It's life.

Writing down the things I'm grateful for is one way to keep me in gratitude.

I don't want to take life for granted. I don't want to take life lessons for granted. I don't want to take people or any of my blessings for granted. I want to be free to live and love. In order to be that person, I must have a grateful heart.

There was a time when I wrote a prayer asking God to help me get back to love, to be filled with grace, to open my heart to love, and to be open to receive love.

Through pain, fear, and brokenness, my heart was so broken I didn't want love anymore. I shut it down. I would certainly long for true love but would only allow so much into my heart. I wouldn't open up fully. It seemed when I would open up, I got hurt, and so what was the point? Later in life, I realized I feared what I wanted most—a true love and loving relationship. I decided I would not do the choosing anymore. It seemed I chose partners that were as broken as I was, if not more. My choices were a direct reflection of what I thought of myself and where I was spiritually.

I have known people who chose their partners based on what they looked like, how much money they had, what they did for a living, their popularity, sexual prowess, or even a seemingly last chance at love. But, none of these things have anything to do with love, real love.

Life lessons come in many forms. I have realized that each lesson, no matter how big or small, is an opportunity for growth. It boils down to our choices. Do we choose to live or to blame? I could have easily wallowed in self-pity, blamed everyone who I, in my most-of-the-time, cloudy perception, thought was the reason for my so-called failed life.

First of all, my life is not a failure. Everyone living has a life. A life is what you do with your days. Your choices. I had to ask myself: am I living my life to the fullest regardless of past hurts? Yes, the guy cheated on the relationship, so what. So what, the guy chose drugs. So what, who I thought was a good friend chose to lie, or the guy who decided rape was okay, or the friend who chose not to help me while I was being raped, and yet another would use me for what they could get from me financially. So many lessons to be learned. There's a myriad of lessons.

I had to get very clear. All these actions were their decisions and choices. They would have to come to terms and deal with the consequences of their actions. As do I. My part in all of these situations is to forgive.

There are people who are miserable. They live their lives blaming everyone. I feel sorry for them (have empathy for them), because they are so busy blaming, they aren't living life to the fullest. Life can be grand, it can be beautiful. But they are so full of hatred, they can't see it. Others are full of drama and living the victim, and just the thought of rising up above the victim is too fearful. So they speak brave while living the traumatized life of a victim. Grateful.

I am as grateful for the things that have been taken as I am for the things I have been given.

It all boils down to this: I have been hurt in many ways, I have hurt others in many ways. Life is filled with the good, bad, and ugly. I have made choices and decisions—some are good, some not so much. Sometimes my emotions run wild.

I have learned through the years to accept life on life's terms. In other words, work with the cards I've been dealt. The serenity prayer is my friend:

> God grant me the serenity to accept the things I cannot change, the courage to change the things I can, and the wisdom to know the difference.

The biggest part (and maybe the hardest) is forgiveness.

I have forgiven all the people who have caused me hurt and harm. I am grateful for the knowledge and wisdom to know how crucial forgiveness is.

Even during the writing of this piece, I felt grateful to be sharing my heart with the world. During the writing there were emotions that began to arise. I did not understand what was going on. I stopped writing because I thought I was headed in the wrong direction. I certainly did not want this writing to be a finger-pointing session, nor did I want it to present me as "poor me, lowly victim." I am not poor, lowly, nor am I a victim. My main point for writing was to share what it was like for me, what happened, and what my life is like today and the process of getting there. I wanted to share the lesson of the event.

I prayed about the writing block. I tried to psychoanalyze what was happening. I talked it over with a few writing partners. I convinced myself to scrap the whole thing and start over. But something was happening within me. It was something important. I could not ignore it. If I wanted healing and revelation, I had to face what was going on. The very first thing I did was get quiet. I wrote about the block. I stopped trying to figure out why it was happening. I accepted it for what it was—a writing block.

One day I attended a women's conference in Dallas, Texas. It was so beautiful. Ladies from all around came in their fancy clothes and beautiful hats. The theme was "Hats off to Women." The venue, the food, the speakers, the singers and the poetess, the attendees, the hostess and mistress of ceremonies were all on point. My heart was full. All of these beautiful sisters in Christ gathering together to honor one another. God was smiling on this event. He was given all the glory! The hostess called out several women who had a special place in her life and heart.

One of the speakers, in giving her testimony, asked a couple of questions: What are you holding on to? What do you need to let go of? I'm paraphrasing because she spoke more to my heart than my head. It was in that moment that something was opened and stirred up within me.

I got emotional. I cried. I tried to carry on as if everything was fine. I even tried to take a selfie. The face I saw looking back at me was not a pretty one. Who was this person? I did not like what I was seeing. I was sinking into a dark space and nothing was stopping it. I said a quick "help me" prayer. The program was over by this time and I headed toward the woman who spoke those words to thank her. I may have looked calm on the outside, but my head was spinning with memories, people, places, and images of me in my early years.

I knew depression was setting in. I did not know the cause. I tried to write about it, but all that ended up on paper were words.

Single words.
  Struggling.
    Darkness.
      Help.

I tried to think of someone to call, but each person I thought of I dismissed for one reason or another. I had my Bible in hand. My bed was filled with devotionals, journals, tissues. I tried to pray. No! I prayed. "Help me." That was good enough. One thing I know for sure, God, my Father, was right there. He promised never to leave or forsake me. He was there holding me as I went through the darkness. Psalm twenty-three kept coming to mind.

What I saw on the surface of my feelings was the image of me when trying to take the selfie at the conference. The person I saw was old, haggard, empty, pained, and saggy.

And oh, did I mention old? I could not get rid of that image. I began to pray, with more words. "Lord, help me see me as you see me." The next day I found out two beautiful spirits, a young girl six years old and a few hours later, another young lady of twenty-one years, both died of a rare cancer. I had been following their lives on Facebook and praying for them.

Did hearing this news feed my darkness? How shallow could I be? Being upset and depressed about aging? I got to a point where I was comparing the selfie image to images of a younger me. Shallow, right? And here two young ladies were no longer with us. Their lives were filled with pain, surgeries, needles, medicine, yet...and yet, through it all, they smiled and laughed and posed for the camera. They loved deeply and cherished their time and all the people in their lives.

There was something going on with me that I did not understand. I kept praying. I began to write in full sentences. Then there was revelation. Yes, what I was going through may have seemed shallow, but it was used to point me to something deeper. Much deeper. It was all about unforgiveness. I had been writing about specific events in my life and the people involved. I thought I had done the work to forgive everyone involved. Maybe I did. But the writing stirred up the ugly stuff and I let it fester. When the question about "what do I need to let go of" came up, the wounds opened as fresh hurts. My image was the ugliness of what unforgiveness looked like.

Old, haggard, empty, pained, saggy, and hurt.

Over the next several hours, the darkness within started to subside. There was some light. I began to feel some semblance of peace. I finally reached out to one of my mentors. She was on a beach somewhere vacationing.

The vision of the vast ocean, the sky, the whole image made me smile. I thanked God for the new image. I thanked Him for the strength I had to reach out. I thanked Him for whatever was happening because I know I would be better on the other side of it. This is gratitude. This is leading life with a grateful heart.

It did not matter what I was going through, my heart remained grateful. I had some overcast days. The darkness was real. The image I saw in that selfie was not real. It was a trick of the enemy! Yet it was useful.

As it's said in a twelve-step program I am a part of, "more will be revealed." There was more work to be done to forgive those who had wronged, harmed, or hurt me. I needed to forgive myself for situations I put myself in. Situations where I may have known were not right for me. Choosing instant gratification over my Father and what I know to be right. He has done for me in one instant more than anyone on earth could ever do in a thousand lifetimes. So I ask myself, why would I choose anyone or anything over Him?

Here I am today in the process of forgiving. I feel good. I am grateful for the experience. This chapter did not follow the plan I had for it. In the midst of writing, God, my Father, intervened and led me on a different path. He wanted me to share a deeper part of me with the world, with you. I've been sharing my testimony of recovery from drugs and alcohol for more than twenty-five years. That's easy most times. I'm accustomed to sharing that story of my life.

Today the story I share is about several things. They may not be evident to you, but they are to me:

- Love myself—I can only give what I have
- Accepting myself and seeing me as God sees me—beautifully and wonderfully made
- God uses everything for my good because I love him and am called for His glory
- Forgiveness is not an event, it's a process—continue the process as long as necessary
- Father answers prayer—He's always on time

- God can change my life direction as He sees fit—it's always for my good and to benefit others
- What I see may not be what I think I'm looking at
- Obedience is better than sacrifice—living a single life that brings Him glory
- It's perfectly okay to honor myself as God's girl

It's time now to write in my gratitude journal. I have so much to choose from. My heart is filled with gratitude and joy. And if I continue to look for things to be grateful for, I'll surely find a boat load! I keep in mind "What I think about, grows." Gratitude! Peace! and Love!

> *Sometimes when you're in a dark place,*
> *You think you've been buried, but*
> *Actually you've been planted.*
> ~ Christine Caine ~

Marsha Sherrill, dynamic life coach, speaker, leadership and personal development coach, and author, believes that as long as you have breath, you can break through to live a life of excellence! Marsha spent more than thirty years in the corporate environment, most of those years as a sales, customer relations, and operations executive. She uses life skills, along with skills learned and utilized in the corporate environment, to become a successful entrepreneur as a coach and inspirational speaker. She coaches people through the process of breakthroughs and blocks. She helps them envision their future, and works with them to develop strategies and goals to realize their dream life and/or potential. She truly loves supporting and helping others to win. Marsha is a life-purpose catalyst and refers to herself as an expert encourager. Visit her website at www.marshasherrill.com.

A GRATEFUL HEART

Sharla J. Vellek

It will feel impossible, like you are dying inside—this is your soul crying out for life. It may take everything you have, every ounce of will and strength. You will lose a part of yourself trying to save something essential and innocent. And when you have given everything, you will recover and you will be set free. You will discover there was even more in you than you ever knew.

– Bryant McGill

I didn't think life could become any more bleak. I was still recovering from a divorce, financially wasn't even making it paycheck to paycheck (a bankruptcy a few years prior making it even more difficult), was a single mom, and a soul filled with codependency and heartbreak. On a good note, I had recently started attending a non-denominational Christian church after telling God to take a hike in college. I was slowly rising back to who God created me to be...and then the phone call came.

It was September 17 at 11:01 p.m. "I am so sorry, honey—he's gone. He's dead." I honestly thought she had been drinking again. I could barely take in her words. My ex-husband of fourteen months had been murdered. As I lay in bed listening, her words became more distant, as if I were in a tunnel. The emotions of grief began to arrive: disbelief, fear, and a numbness that would not leave for months. I thought about the child we had together and then more emotions found their way into my mind. How do I tell Dalton? What do I share with him? How was I going to do this alone? And then a shame-filled thought—I no longer had someone to blame for Dalton's poor behavior, if it ever arose. Wow! I had to dispel that one quickly. What a horrible thought!

Dalton and I dressed to go be with my ex-husband's family, but there was nothing we could do. Very little was known other than the police were on the scene...his home...his bedroom. We came back to our apartment, calling my parents who arrived in the middle of the night...my parents who became and still are my wise rocks. In the weeks to come, our lives forever changed and I was on auto pilot. Memorial arrangements, cremation, rumors, lost friendships, investigations, federal marshals, victims' advocacy, Social Security, attorneys, autopsy report, picking up his belongings, haggling with his employer over life insurance benefits, more attorneys, trying to arrange appointments with the Dougy Center... and amidst all of this, my emotions pushed to the forefront. I knew I could no longer avoid facing them.

It began with JUDGMENT. I had full-blown judgment going on with my ex. He was a drinker, a lover of life, his world filled with friendships, baseball, and beer—he was always living "Life by the Drop." When he died, I truly didn't know if he was going to heaven or hell. All I knew was, I didn't want to lie to our son. I wanted to be able to tell him where his dad would end up, if he would ever see him again. At his memorial, standing before his urn filled with his ashes, I simply asked God to show me the truth of Duane's final destination so I could share the truth with Dalton.

Later that week, I went to my ex-husband's home to pick up his belongings, as Dalton was his heir. As I was going through his belongings, I found his wallet and inside was a card with these words on it: *Dear Father in heaven. Thank you for loving me. I admit that I have sinned against you. Please forgive me of my sins. I believe Jesus is the Son of God and that He paid for all my sins with His blood on the Cross. I invite Jesus into my life to walk with me each day. I accept His sacrifice for me and His forgiveness of my sins. Because of my confession and His free gift of eternal life I will go to be with Him when I die. Thank you again for loving me. Amen.* My eyes became pools of tears. Not just because God had answered my prayer at the memorial for the truth, but because I had judged my ex based upon what I saw externally, not what was in his heart. I was brought to my knees that day, recognizing how broken I was. Today, I carry this card in my wallet, a daily reminder as it whispers the truth of God's love. A reminder that God can open our eyes, change our perspective, and to not assume or judge, but to see the beautiful hearts of all men.

The second emotion was FORGIVENESS. The months that followed Duane's death were mixed with healing and court dates. I spent many lunch hours at work soaking in God's sacred presence, in His word. Highlighting, praying, and crying. I remember the waves of grief that would come, and I would run to the bathroom, sitting on the floor, crying—just letting it all out. Begging God to make time pass, to make it all go away.

As time moved on, the victims advocate shared that we had a choice to speak in court to the men that killed Duane. I knew in my heart I would choose to do this, but I also knew I needed to forgive them before this happened. Again, much time, tears, and prayers were spent on this topic.

Then one day, on my way to work, it hit me like a freight train. As Mac Powell's voice filled the air with the song "Thief," I realized what I had done. Once again my heart had been filled with judgement. Did I not get it the first time? I had to pull my car over—the realization came so fast, it shook my soul. I began to sob. It was that moment when everything that had been building up let go. I realized then that I was no better than the man who had wrapped his hands around Duane's neck. I, too, had ended a life through abortion several years prior. Mac's words continued to fill the air, speaking from the viewpoint of the thief crucified with Christ, begging Him to remember him when He came to His kingdom. The lyrics spoke of love, compassion, repentance, forgiveness...life everlasting.

Just as Jesus forgave the thief, I knew he had forgiven me. Both of us had sinned, both of us forgiven. I knew then that I could also forgive the men that killed my ex. I knew that the forgiveness was not about accepting what they did; it was about healing my soul. The judge and God would decide the final punishment for these men and my memories were mine. As I sat in the car trying to control the sobbing, I recalled the parable in the Bible about the woman who had been suffering from bleeding for twelve years. God healed her because of her faith. God shared with me that we all sin. Everyone should be extended forgiveness. It is our job to forgive, to not judge and to love.

The final emotion was LOVE. Mark 12:30 says: "Love the Lord your God with all your heart and with all your soul and with all your mind and with all your strength. The second is this: Love your neighbor as yourself. There is no commandment greater than these" (NIV). My first thoughts, thoughts of my carnal mind, were "pure garbage"...how could I love these men? And if this was God's law, what exactly was He talking about?

Shame is a powerful emotion. It can paralyze you. I had a lot of shame surrounding my abortion. So much so that when I chose to write about my "rock bottom," I had forgotten about this key component of healing. When I realized what I had done, I was filled with shame as only a few know. I knew by sharing this story, I would need to let the world know. I knew I had to write about it.

Healing, release of any shame, letting go.

I did not have much of a grateful heart during that first year after Duane died. It was more like trying to claw my way up from the bottom of a cave without a rope. Always seeing the light, the hope, God, but grasping for anything to get me there. However, through this journey, my heart was opened and I allowed Love to heal it. It broke open a gratefulness for life itself, thus giving me a grateful heart.

I began to take long walks with my son, breathing in crisp air, the smell of fall leaves, wood smoke, listening to birds chat with each other. I became grateful for these simple joys. These hard lessons of judgment, forgiveness, and love would be the rock bottom foundation of what my soul would journey and need in the coming years. I saw the difficulties of blending a family, of prayerfully creating a friendship with his ex-wife, the ongoing journey my son walks with the death of his dad and his auditory memory diagnosis. There has been the diagnosis of my youngest son at age four with retinoblastoma (a childhood eye cancer) and ultimately losing his eye to cancer. I've experienced the coming out of my oldest son and finally the demise of my second marriage.

Life is filled with heartache and trauma. It is messy. We have a choice as to how to respond and how to look at life. Is your heart filled with joy and gratefulness? Somehow through all of the heartache, He taught me to see the beauty around me, that it takes the storm to create the rainbow, the rain to grow a garden. I take this in moment by moment. Sometimes it is still difficult. I get pulled in by the drama of life, yet He always shows up—always guiding me to a grateful heart.

Always reminding me to choose joy.

> *The reality is that you will grieve forever. You will not 'get over' the loss of a loved one; you will learn to live with it. You will heal and you will rebuild yourself around the loss you have suffered. You will be whole again, but you will never be the same. Nor should you be the same, nor would you want to.* – Elizabeth Kubler-Ross and John Kessler

Sharla Vellek has a passion to create harmonious, meaningful relationships with the community around her, leading her to create a foundation for moms of children with cancer to have a weekend self-care getaway. Sharla partnered with Momcology.org in 2014 to expand her foundation, placing the retreats as a program of Momcology. Her personal journeys of sorrow, divorce, losing her first son's father to a violent crime, her second son being diagnosed with retinoblastoma (a rare form of childhood eye cancer), and much more led Sharla to seek God's joy and blessings in each moment and live a life blessed by grace. Sharla lives in Vancouver, Washington with her two boys, their labradoodle Zoe, and spends time running, camping, reading, traveling, and hanging out with friends.

THE DOOR OF FREEDOM SWUNG WIDE OPEN

Angie Webb

Such a person feeds on ashes; a deluded heart misleads him; he cannot save himself, or say, "Is this thing in my right hand a lie?"

– Isaiah 44:20 (NIV)

Living with fear and anxiety most of my life led me down a path that hindered everyone around me, and my life was not really being lived.

I only survived. Living was possible for everyone else but me. I had struggled with fear since the early age of around four years old.

Looking at life through a clouded lens allowed life to become very blurred over time. I so wanted to have freedom to travel, go shopping, visit my extended family in other towns, and be involved with my children's outside activities. Yet the fear and agoraphobia kept me bound to the enemy.

The choices made for me by others in my childhood allowed the enemy to gain a foothold early on in life. The enemy knew exactly how to keep me bound up, which allowed fear to become my best friend, and often only friend. As a believer in the Lord and a Christian since the age of ten, God had saved me for a reason, or so I thought.

No matter how I struggled or how much I begged, borrowed, and pleaded with the Lord for healing in some form of a miracle, it was always elusive...just out of reach.

Searching for freedom was so difficult when I could look around and see everyone else functioning normally in everyday aspects of life such as driving alone, going to Walmart alone, or even staying home alone. Those certainly were not things I could ever do in the depths of my agoraphobic life and the constant panic attacks.

Why did God seem to think I was strong enough to carry such a burden? Hadn't I already faced enough as a young child constantly having words of despair, disregard, and discouragement spoken over me? Wasn't my life of having two family members lost to suicide as well as one to murder enough? Why this as well?

Agoraphobia is classified in the American Psychological Association as: An extreme fear of being in public places or open spaces from which escape may be difficult or embarrassing

It certainly was not God's best for me, but it was the life I was given to live. During the worst of times, I became suicidal and often wanted to crawl into a hole and never return. Life was hard and lonely.

How do you overcome something you have had from the earliest memories of your childhood?

I had no idea how to free myself, yet I continued to pray and seek God and His Word. I continued to claim His promises He had for ME, as well as seek counseling for the past harm done and the loss of my family due to suicides and murder.

Every day was a day of deciding what I could and couldn't do. Some days would allow a small trip to the local grocery store or a clothing store, but certainly not a trip to Walmart or a drive out of town alone. At the worst point in my struggle, I had not driven to the next town over or outside my own town's city limits alone in over fifteen years. I could barely ride in the car while my husband drove to the next town over thirty miles away without having constant panic attacks. I know it is hard to understand, but this was my life.

After a health crisis in 2008, the agoraphobia became all-consuming and overpowering, even more so than the previous thirty years before. Something that at first I was able to control somewhat now had become even more powerful. Life was never easy for me, but now it was so, so hard. Even walking outside to the mailbox was fearful and overpowering. I had no clue as to why the bondage was so much more controlling because I continued seeking God and His Word. However, whatever I was doing wasn't working.

During the depths of the worst days, my mother-in-law would come stay with me while my husband went to his job. It was hard having a "babysitter," yet that was what my life required at the time. We would play board games, watch television, or spend time talking, but each day was difficult regardless if I was alone or with someone. The panic attacks were so powerful and came about for no apparent reason. I could not understand it myself so I couldn't explain to anyone else my struggles.

Over the course of six months, I totally quit leaving my home, even for church or grocery shopping. I lived and breathed every moment of every day inside my house. It was such a sad life, but it was also a sad life for my family. I had no identity any longer other than one who could not function alone, sleep at night panic-attack free, or leave her home. My kids suffered, as did my marriage. Every relationship suffered and no one understood. More importantly, I did not understand and doubted God was even listening to me. If He was listening, He sure didn't seem to want to help me—or so it seemed.

My faith suffered during this time and eventually I just gave up. I developed a very one-sided view of the world, which meant that the world revolved around my needs, all the while pushing everyone else away. Life was lonely and certainly not what I had envisioned for myself. As a child, I had huge dreams for my life such as becoming president of the United States, or a seismologist, or an author, yet none of that was coming to fruition.

After many months of struggling due to my health crisis, I finally located a very caring doctor who listened to my desperate cries. It took all of my faith just to arrive at his office for a visit because I couldn't even ride in a vehicle during this time without panic attacks. The doctor ordered some medication to help with the panic attacks as well as for sleep deprivation. Over a period of a few weeks, I could feel some "control" returning, but certainly not total freedom or healing. That freedom and healing was something I never believed would happen in my life, yet somewhere deep inside hope remained and I continued to pray and believe God was listening (Psalm 73:26).

For four years, life went on just as it had before. Some days of a little freedom and some days of overwhelming pain, struggle, and feelings of defeat.

During those four years, I began to write about my journey of loss of family to suicides and murder, as well as my struggle with agoraphobia. These previous articles can be found at http://joyfuljourneynewsletter. blogspot.com. This helped me deal with some of the feelings I was facing, but was also a way to support others.

In 2012, I had finally felt more comfortable with myself and found some inklings of freedom from the past struggles from childhood and young adulthood, much through counseling with a wonderful therapist. Facing the past allowed my future to become more optimistic, as well as putting the proper perspective on past harm and pain. Small glimpses of freedom were on the horizon, yet often the little devil would once again get me sidetracked.

My only living grandmother was turning ninety-five in January of that year, yet we had not seen each other for more than nine years due to my anxiety and agoraphobia. I so desperately wanted to visit her once again before the end of her life, but I had no idea how I would make a nine-hour trip when I couldn't even drive across town. I was afraid if I didn't make this trip to visit her, I would not see her again on this side of heaven, yet the fear, anxiety, and agoraphobia always kept me so bound up that any type of freedom seemed impossible. The enemy certainly knew how to always speak just the right words for me to give up again. Round and round I went, always reverting to what was comfortable.

My often only friend had one name: Fear.

The summer of 2012, I attended a woman's conference at a local church. This was an experience filled with fear, panic, and stress because I had to drive to the church alone and at night, which I didn't ever do. When I arrived at the church, I knew that there was a spirit within the church walls that was so comforting as well as uplifting. Even though I had never attended this church, I felt somewhat at peace there.

As we were beginning the worship service, two older ladies walked up to me and asked if they could pray for me, which of course I agreed to. As they were praying, I could sense that God was doing a work in my heart and life. These two women were part of the healing journey that began that summer day in 2012. It was one that I never expected to happen, but so it began.

As the weekend of the conference progressed, I felt more and more alive, but also more at peace with myself, my life, and the plans God had for me. It was something I had never felt before. Prayers continued through the weekend as women shared their journeys of life. Some were hard and some were good, yet all the while we gave praise to the Lord for His continued love, blessings, and protection.

The days after the conference I told my husband that I could sense a difference in my life, but I was unsure of exactly what it meant. We continued to pray as we always had for some form of healing or miracle in my life so that I was truly FREE. Each day I would pray and claim the promises I previously claimed daily, yet on one particular day God prompted me to read Isaiah 44:20 where He says when we feed on ashes and believe the lie in our right hand, we are living a life that is not as He intended. This is a scripture I had read before, but on that particular day, God spoke to me about all of the fear, the past, the spoken words of abuse, the agoraphobia...on and on. It was all ASHES and LIES. It was not from Him but from the enemy. I sat there stunned as I read this verse because I had never thought of it that way. He was getting right to the core of my thinking and it was not what I had believed it to be. I had always thought the fear, anxiety, agoraphobia, and my past harm as a child was all I would ever have, and that it was the "thorn" I was called to carry in this life. Yet, here He was speaking something totally different to my heart.

When my husband arrived home from work that day, I asked him about this verse and if what I was sensing in my spirit made sense. He agreed with what I had heard in my heart, and thus began the journey out of fear, anxiety, and agoraphobia. The path to freedom was going to require some form of action on my part for the reality of healing to be true in my life. Freedom was certainly not anything I expected to experience in my lifetime, so this was a "miracle" in more than one way.

In August of 2012, my family and I took our first vacation in over fifteen years to visit my family nine hours away. The first few hours on the road were very difficult, and at the halfway point of the trip, I began to cry uncontrollably. My husband and son were concerned and both began to worry because I was so upset. They believed I was having a severe panic attack, but after I explained to them that they were tears of joy, I began to experience a feeling of bricks falling off of my shoulders. Bricks that had kept me bound to fear, shame, guilt, anxiety, and agoraphobia and abuse were all falling away slowly as we continued down the highway. Each mile offered a little more peace in myself as well as the circumstances I found myself in, whether it was on the highway, at a restaurant, or shopping with family, I felt more comfortable being away from home, all the while enjoying time with family.

After the first vacation, my husband and I have had three more trips, each of which has allowed more and more freedom. God has done a tremendous work, and I am forever thankful for the plans He continues to unfold before me, all of which are for good and for His purpose. Even in the midst of struggle, God is always walking beside us, holding our hand, all the while listening to our desperate cries. Please do not give up on your miracle because it may be just around the corner. Keep praying and believing because I am proof that God is never done with our story.

Angie Webb can be found at http://angiekaywebb.com where she offers hope, encouragement, and love to others struggling with fear, anxiety, or agoraphobia. She shares her journey of more than thirty years as well as the loss of several family members to suicide and murder. Angie has a compassionate heart and loves to connect with her readers. You can also contact Angie for speaking and writing at the above address.

ROCK BOTTOM IS A BEAUTIFUL PLACE 3

NOT ONE THING

Mia A. Williams

If you have been feeling isolated in a dark place, don't worry. God did not bury you, He planted you! He is just cultivating you and growing you. Seeds root in the dark place; destiny evolves in the dark place; transformation occurs in the dark place. I pray for your endurance in this planting season. In due season you will reap the harvest.

– Bishop T.D. Jakes

Not the Bathroom!

I'd gotten home from work with one thing on my mind: rest. It was a Friday evening and I just wanted to unwind. My boyfriend, on the other hand, had different plans. He arrived home about an hour after me, grinning from ear to ear, obviously excited about something.

"Get dressed," he said.

He wanted to go out on the town and I wasn't having it. I tried the power of persuasion. "Let's just order a pizza and watch movies until we pass out." When that didn't work, I tried whining, but it had no effect.

"Get dressed, we're going out."

I just flat out refused. Once he realized that I wasn't going to budge, he gave up on trying to coax me out of the house and went into our bedroom. When he came back into the living room, he said something odd, "You left the candle burning in the bathroom near a towel. You're going to burn the place down."

I thought, *Well why didn't you just blow it out?*

I leapt from the couch and ran to the bathroom. I figured I must have lit the candle and forgotten about it. Looking at the counter top, I could see the candle wasn't burning and the wax was still hard. Before I had a chance to say anything, I heard him say, "You don't see it?"

And suddenly, there it was: a diamond engagement ring sparkling from its box sitting on the counter. I grabbed the box and spun around. Harold was kneeling between our bedroom and the master bath, and with tears forming in his eyes, he asked, "Will you marry me?" I think I was partially shocked as I stammered through a yes. Then I thought, *not the bathroom!* I promised myself that from that moment on, anytime he told me to get dressed to go out, I would do so, no questions asked.

Three Weeks to Plan

One thing I've always loved about Harold is when he puts his mind to something, he really commits to it. He was pretty set on getting married immediately, and in living right and being in accordance with God's will – I completely agreed. We'd both just recently relocated to Texas and had been living together for the last three months. We both wanted to get married and I was having a bad case of baby fever. On Friday night, we sent text messages to our families saying that we were engaged. By Saturday morning, those messages had changed to:

> *We're getting married next month on Saturday, March 23. We know this is late notice. We will have a small ceremony now and bigger one later. Please let us know if you can make it. P.S. No, we are not pregnant.*

Exactly one month from the day we got engaged, we were going to tie the knot. For the sake of time and money we decided to keep it a small and intimate affair; I had three weeks to plan.

In the weeks leading up to our wedding, we attended premarital counseling sessions with our pastor in private (we'd already found and joined a church), and also a group session with other couples from our church. We fasted and watched *The Bible* series every Sunday evening while working out at the gym. We picked out a cake together, and Harold even picked out my wedding dress after my mom told me the dress I'd originally chosen "looked like a bird." (That's a long story for another day and time.) With the help of my best friends I was able to find a local photographer and make-up artist, order a bouquet, and choose a place for dinner after the ceremony. In a whirlwind of happiness, nothing could have prepared me for what was coming...

Cancelled

I woke early on the morning of March twenty-third and lay in bed listening to the birds chirping from the tree nearby. It was a peaceful morning and I could smell the fresh rain that had fallen over night. I was calm and at peace. Several of my girlfriends sent me text messages to say congratulations. When I replied to one of my friends that it had rained early that morning, she replied that the rain was, "God's tears of joy." I, too, had joy as I began to get ready.

I'm not the least bit superstitious about seeing the bride before the wedding, so Harold and I stayed in our apartment the night before our wedding. We had two bedrooms and two full bathrooms, so getting ready at the same time wouldn't be a hassle. I had an endless to-do list and was trying to grab everything I needed before my best friends arrived to take me to the hairdresser.

As I bustled around the house, I suddenly had this odd feeling. It was like this sudden awareness that the atmosphere felt thick and tense and cold – the exact opposite of the peace I had felt only an hour earlier. Something was terribly wrong. At first I tried to shake it off as nervousness or perhaps a case of cold feet. I even joked with myself that maybe it really was bad luck for us to see each other on our wedding day. I decided that the best thing would be to just ask Harold if everything was okay. I took him by the hand and led him to the couch. "What's wrong?"

Before I could blink something bubbled over and erupted and we were in a full-blown argument. We went from one to one hundred in a matter of seconds, and I couldn't control or stop what was happening. We were in the living room screaming and hurling words at one another that didn't seem to make any sense. It was like an out of body experience watching us verbally spar—eyes wide, nostrils flailing, gestures wild and exaggerated. This was not the picture you'd expect to see of two people who loved each other and were only hours away from getting married. Nothing made sense...

I can't remember what the argument was about or even the exact words that were said, with the exception of four awful words that slammed into me like a freight train, "THE WEDDING IS OFF!" I stood there dazed, feeling like my oxygen had been cut off. Somewhere in the distance I heard the door slam. Then my phone began to vibrate—my best friends had arrived to take me to the hairdresser.

Intervention

The next few hours were honestly some of the worst hours of my life. I was too embarrassed to tell my two best friends what had occurred.

I went to the hairdresser and got my hair done pretending everything was okay. When my parents called me, I assumed it was to soothe and console me but instead we ended up yelling and arguing also: *You're too stubborn, Mia. You don't listen, Mia.* I kept thinking, *Please God, let this be a nightmare.* But even my worst nightmares had never been this bad.

Our parents staged a sort of "intervention." In reality, it felt more like an ambush. It seemed like everyone had heard Harold's thoughts and feelings and no one—not even my own family—cared to hear my point of view or how I was feeling. This was the furthest thing from a fairy-tale wedding I could possibly imagine.

To get on to the most important parts of the story, let me summarize the rest: after much prayer and guidance from both sides of our family, we decided to get married. The rest of the day felt surreal, dream-like... perfunctory: getting dressed, cameras snapping, a quick ceremony, forced smiles, awkward toasts and tears of... joy?

The Dark Place

I am a very private person. My need to be private sometimes gives others the perception that my life is somehow perfect and that I never experience heartaches and pains. The truth is I often suffer in silence. I am stoic and strong for others when helping them through their situations, but I often carry my own burdens alone, sharing them only with God.

The story of my wedding day will be shocking to most of my family. I've never told this story to anyone and have kept it hidden in the deepest depths of my heart and mind. Even my best friends don't really know what happened because I shielded them from most of the mess. I know they must have had so many questions, yet knowing and respecting who I am, they didn't press me for answers. I will forever love them for this.

After my wedding, I was truly in a dark place. On the outside, I was a façade of happiness. On the inside, my emotions were a raging tornado of anger, humiliation, shame, embarrassment, hurt, disbelief, confusion and bitterness. I pretended that my wedding day was the happiest day of my life, to the point of lying when people asked me how my wedding day was and even writing "The Happiest Day of My Life" in my wedding scrapbook. It was hard for me to even enjoy the weddings of our friends and family. I would struggle with jealousy and thoughts like: *Why did this awful thing have to happen to me? Didn't I deserve a happy wedding? She looks so happy; why couldn't my wedding day be like hers?*

On bad days I would look at Harold and think, *why did I get married?* On *really* bad days I would contemplate divorce. It took me a long time to forgive my husband and to trust him with my heart.

It was in this dark place that my greatest transformation occurred and where God delivered me from the torment of my feelings and from being crippled by shame and bitterness. It was here that God showed me the freedom that comes with forgiveness. And eventually, God gave me peace concerning that day.

Gratitude

I serve an amazing God! He has taken the tragedy of that day and turned it into triumph! God has shown me that I no longer need to hide behind my wedding day and pretend that everything was okay. My wedding day was a hot mess! But God has turned my experience into an opportunity for growth and maturity and a newfound transparency that I did not have before.

One of my greatest lessons was in forgiveness. What I've learned about forgiveness is that it isn't for the person who wronged you, it's for you! Forgiveness doesn't make what happened right, it doesn't mean you are condoning or excusing the actions of others, nor should offering forgiveness depend on the other person acknowledging what happened or apologizing. Forgiveness does not mean that I have to forget what happened: it means I've made a decision to not be bitter or angry or to let what occurred control my thoughts, emotions, or actions. It means that I am following God's commandment to possess a forgiving spirit just as I seek forgiveness for my wrongs.

God has delivered me from the need to create a perception of perfection. The new me is transparent and open to sharing all the ugly, dark places and, most importantly, in accepting God's forgiveness and His transforming grace. I no longer live in shame, guilt, or fear of embarrassment. I have learned that God uses every part of our story for His glory, and that nothing we go through is in vain. God will take every painful, embarrassing, or shameful moment and turn it into something good!

> *And we know that all things work together for good to them that love God, to them who are called according to his purpose.*
> *– Romans 8:28*

Not One Thing!

I saw a post on Facebook that said, "If you could go back in time and change one thing from your wedding ceremony, what would it be?" Previously my response would have been obvious, but today, with a joyous heart, I can say, **NOT ONE THING!** My experience has brought me tremendous growth and maturity and a powerful lesson in forgiveness and living in shame. I am humbled by God's grace and the way He uses our worst experiences to draw out the best in us!

Harold and I surrendered the broken pieces of our marriage to God and let Him completely transform our union. We continue to invest in our marriage by serving God and keeping Him first in all aspects of our lives; by taking time out just for us (date nights!); and by surrounding ourselves with other married couples ready to impart godly wisdom when we stumble or lose our way.

Don't get me wrong, we still have our struggles, but we strive to make sure that our conflicts end in forgiveness; in us drawing closer together; in deeper respect and understanding for one another; and an even greater intimacy. God gets all the glory for the leaps and bounds we have made in our marriage, for my husband's support in sharing our story, and for the impact we hope this story will have on others. As one of our dear friends shared with us after our wedding, "It doesn't matter how the day started. It matters how it ended."

Our story will continue to evolve long after our wedding photos have faded and my wedding dress has turned yellow with age. I pray that our story blesses you and that, like me, you realize that you don't need to hide behind shame or pretend to live a perfect life.

Mia A. Williams, MBA is a passionate leader, faithful servant, avid reader, life enthusiast, and lover of all things fabulous. An ever-evolving teacher and student, she teaches business courses online and believes that God is ordering her steps to pursue her PhD in Leadership Studies. Affectionately known as "Mamma Mia," she is known to take charge and pave the way, determined to live each day placing her all on the altar. Mia is passionate about encouraging women from all walks of life to live their best lives while unabashedly basking in the grace of God. She divides her time between serving God and her community, spending time with her family, continuously learning, traveling, and creating beautiful things. Mia lives in Texas with her beloved husband and son. Join the Women of Grace movement at www.thewomenofgrace.com

AFTERWORD

Are you amazed at the glory of God? His grace? His power? How He takes our broken pieces and uses every single one of them to help others?

My prayer is that you have been inspired by the real women who have shared their real stories. Real, authentic, gut-level, honest truth.

Women just like you.

Many of the women in here struggled with sharing their stories. These are not easy stories to read. They were even harder stories to write. But as they shared, as they wrestled with their words, with their insecurities, and with their fears, something amazing happened.

They were set free in so many ways.

We know that Rock Bottom is a beautiful place.

We know that we walk forward from here in the strength of God and our shared sisterhood in Christ.

We pray this over you and your story, that it will bring you closer to the God who loves you.

Prayer Of St. Francis

Lord make me a channel of thy peace—that where there is hatred, I may bring love—that where there is wrong, I may bring the spirit of forgiveness—that where there is discord, I may bring harmony—that where there is error, I may bring truth—that where there is doubt, I may bring faith—that where there is despair, I may bring hope—that where there are shadows, I may bring light—that where there is sadness, I may bring joy.

Lord, grant that I may seek rather to comfort than to be comforted—to understand, than to be understood—to love, than to be loved.

For it is by self-forgetting that one finds. It is by forgiving that one is forgiven. It is by dying that one awakens to Eternal Life. Amen.

God is good. We are delighted that you are with us on this journey.

We encourage you to reach out to us:

- www.rockbottomisabeautifulplace.com
- Visit each woman's website
- Friend them on Facebook

When you feel like you have hit the bottom, trust God.

Look up.

Ask for help.

Surrender.

Give Him your broken empty worn out heart. He is waiting for you and He loves you so very much!

You are beautiful in your brokenness.

ABOUT
DIANE CUNNINGHAM

Diane Cunningham, M.Ed. is the President and Founder of the *National Association of Christian Women Entrepreneurs®*, a global association for women to connect, create, and collaborate through monthly online training, conferences, networking, and business strategies. NACWE was launched in May 2010 and has been building and expanding since that time with members throughout the United States, Canada, and beyond. This community and sisterhood is the premier place to learn marketing and mindset in a faith foundation.

In 2014, she added the *Christian Women's Leadership Institute*™ to train women to become Certified Group Facilitators and to raise up leaders around the world.

Diane is also a consultant, author, video guru, artist, plane crash survivor, and former master's level therapist. She has a Master's Degree in Education (guidance and counseling) from Whitworth College in Spokane, Washington and a bachelor's degree from the same school in interpersonal communications.

Diane is an Amazon Best Selling author of the book series *"Rock Bottom is a Beautiful Place"* and *"The Inspired Business Toolkit,"* along with *"Dear Female Entrepreneur, My Friend."* She also co-authored *"Inspired Women Succeed"* with Jo Ann Fore. Her next book about her personal journey and brave adventures will come out at the end of 2015.

She currently lives in Grapevine, Texas with her cat Zander where she drinks too much coffee, eats way too many bacon cheeseburgers, and paints "Heart Art by Diane" in her kitchen. She is single, sassy, and sober. She has found the gift of serenity. She trusts God completely.

Diane's mission is this: To inspire women to dream big, catch on fire, and change the world.

Connect with Diane at www.facebook.com/DianeCunninghamFriends andwww.facebook.com/NACWE for fun updates, silly videos, lively conversation and great ACT FAST NOW business mentoring.

Find her at www.dianecunningham.com or www.nacwe.org.

JOIN OUR NACWE FAMILY!

Are you a woman that has the dream of starting a business?

Or a woman who has been successful in business, but lacking the support of a group of like-minded friends?

Are you a Christian entrepreneur tired of being alone with your standards, ethics, and values?

We know how you feel....

- Are you wondering where to begin?
- Fearful of asking for the sale?
- Do you struggle with social media?
- Are you totally overwhelmed with your list of to-do's?
- Struggling to figure out if you need to hire help and who to hire?
- Feeling isolated as you work alone or as the boss of a small group?

Or you might be...

- Undercharging for your services
- Overwhelmed by technology
- Afraid of being "salesy"
- Know you need a better system, but have no idea what that means

You have found the right place!

At NACWE, we "get it" and we "get you"! We get you because we are YOU!

The National Association of Christian Women Entrepreneurs was born out of a passion to connect women who are ready to create, collaborate, and contribute to changing the world. We gather people and ideas together through online content, tele-courses, individual/group coaching and retreats. Our desire is to unite under a common goal of helping one another to succeed and thrive in business. We are blessed to share in a common faith in Jesus Christ, and yet know that we might each choose to worship in a different way.

Get **connected** to Christian women entrepreneurs throughout the United States and Canada for networking, business building, and prayer support.

Start **creating** new ideas, plans, programs, and products with help from our valuable monthly training calls and webinars.

Begin **collaborating** with women who can walk beside you on the journey with love and not competition.

Visit us at www.nacwe.org to get started with your membership today!

INVITE DIANE TO SPEAK

Inspiring Heart-Based Businesswomen To Infinite Success

Diane Cunningham is a gifted communicator who offers inspiration, motivation, and encouragement to all those who come into her path. Her genuine transparency comes through in the insightful examples she gives her audiences as she helps them to create a life filled with passion and purpose. She loves to provide inspiration strategies for business groups, weekend gatherings, or corporate retreats.

As a speaker, Diane facilitates interactive discussions, along with providing useful and thought-provoking information for seminars, networking events, and women's retreats in the church and corporate realm. She is also available for corporate training events and keynotes.

> *"Diane Cunningham is an engaging, enlightening, speaker. Her powerful, heartfelt message is full of substance, easily remembered, and when implemented, inspires women to a higher level of success. It is with the greatest of confidence that I recommend Diane Cunningham."* – Julie Ziglar Norman, Founder of Ziglar Women, *Guideposts* author, international inspirational speaker, www.ZiglarWomen.com

Diane speaks to groups of:

- Christian women in business
- Entrepreneurs
- Chamber of Commerce members
- Direct sales companies
- Leaders

Most Requested Presentations:

- Inspired Business Secrets: Marketing Tools to Generate Leads, Increase Revenue, and Build a Thriving Community!

- Act Fast Now: Jumpstart Your Business with the A.C.T.I.O.N. Formula for Success

- Learn How to Catapult Your Business with Heart-Based Communities

- Rock Bottom Is A Beautiful Place

Contact Diane at diane@dianecunningham.com or visit http://nacwe.org/speaking/ to discuss the ideal program for your next event.

Are you looking for a business coach who shares your passion, enthusiasm, and faith? Go to

http://dianecunningham.com/pickmybrain/

and fill out the information form. Diane will schedule a Get Acquainted Session so you can discuss your options for private coaching.

COACHING WITH DIANE CUNNINGHAM

- Do you need more clients so you can get into higher profits and help your family?

- Are you sick and tired of lying awake at night feeling overwhelmed and like you are never going to "arrive?"

- Are you ready to finally use your God-given gifts and strengths to make more money and start supporting the causes you are passionate about?

- Do you need accountability, guidance, and tough love to stop HIDING OUT and really build a business empire?

In addition to the membership options at the National Association of Christian Women Entrepreneurs, Diane coaches a select number of clients each year, privately and in small mastermind groups.

She provides coaching in person, through Skype, by phone, and at retreat locations. She offers VIP days that get you unstuck, focused, and into action.

If you do not have someone inspiring, uplifting, supporting, and holding a bigger vision for you than you hold for yourself, you will benefit greatly from the one-on-one coaching with Diane.

This is the program to get intense feedback, personalized research, step-by-step training, and accountability. We will work together generating ideas, fixing broken places, thinking of taglines, researching your competition, and helping you to "move the needle."

With her background as a counselor and now as a "business therapist," she helps you work through challenges, mindset struggles, and unhealthy business habits. We create a strategic solution-focused action plan for success in your marketing and your mindset. And we pray at the beginning and end of every session.

The type of client that she loves to work with is:

- An action taker

- Willing to try new things

- Committed to working through the discomfort of change and growth

- On a mission to build the business that God has given them

- Ready to let go of mistaken beliefs and mindsets

Are you ready to get started and discuss the right program for you?

Go to http://dianecunningham.com/pickmybrain/ and fill out the form or email diane@dianecunningham.com.